PRAISE FOR JOE WENKE'S

PAPAL BULL

"I may burn in hell for even having read this book." *John C. Wood*

"If you enjoyed Wenke's take on the Bible, *You Got to Be Kidding!* read his exegesis of the Catholic Church's past two thousand years. . . . Mordantly funny, scrupulously researched." *E. B. Boatner, Lavender Magazine*

"If you wonder why a 'merciful' God created a no-exit-ever hell or if you entertain thoughts of how boring the traditional religious notion of heaven might be, you will meet a savagely witty ally in Wenke's book." *Joe Meyers, CTPost*

"Joe Wenke is an extraordinary writer. . . . This book is an enlightening journey (for both the author and the reader) that was tenderly written by an exceptional person who is not afraid to let others know about what occurs in so many families, causing a great deal of pain and uncertainty. It is something that should be read by anyone and everyone, regardless of their religion or how they were raised/told by others to believe. There are no words to express the depth of my gratitude to Mr. Wenke and I will be anxiously awaiting any other material that he wishes to write, because I am a lifelong fan." *Jules*

"I absolutely LOVED this book. . . . I highly recommend it to any Catholic who is considering recovering from his condition." *Philip G. Harding*

D1563461

"Ex-Catholics will love this book. It is an amazing satire of the Catholic Church. Every bit as funny as *You Got To Be Kidding!* I highly recommend." *Holly Michele*

"I love this book! It is not only informative but funny as hell." *Rick Martin*

"Funny, clever and spot on." *V. Kennedy*

"Whew! I feel like I've been to confession with the universe, (not God, that's a bad fairytale) and I've been absolved of . . . something. Thank you, Dr. Wenke, for putting into words . . . what I've been thinking about religion, especially Catholicism for a long time. . . . The one thought that kept repeating for me throughout the book, was that I need to buy about 2 dozen copies of this and hand them out to my family members, and at least try to spark a conversation." *Deborah*

"Papal Bull is brilliant and funny, well-researched and informative. . . . [Wenke] writes with humor that is at once scathing, insightful and absurd. His recounting of stories from Catholic grade school made me laugh out loud." *Lori Giampa*

"A cutting, satirical look at Catholic beliefs regarding saints, Mary, birth control, the treatment of women, and of course the huge scandalous cover-up of molestation." *Tiffany A. Harkleroad*

"Impeccably researched and sharply written. . . . [Wenke's] wit and incisive perspective consistently deliver humor and important points to anyone willing to open their minds. . . . A work in which you can think, laugh, and ask the important questions is a must-read." *David Nor*

"For some reason, I kept falling into a George Carlin voice as I read the book." *Joseph Spuckler*

"I love the cover and I love the term 'recovering Catholic' of which I believe I am one. I think any one who went to Catholic School in the fifties and sixties . . . probably had many of the same experiences that the author describes from his school years." *Diane Scholl*

A great and sometimes funny book all 'recovering Catholics' should read. In fact it should be required reading for anybody who considers themselves Holy. Brilliant insight & questions every Catholic should ask themselves." *Robert Kennemer*

"It is necessary to call the church out on their horrendous errors and this book is much needed in society. . . . Papal Bull is timely and makes for some very interesting reading. Enjoy!" *Lynda Smock*

"I not only laughed a great deal, but [the book] also gave me a lot to think about." *Michele Barbrow*

"A must read. Excellent!" *Carole*

"This satirical book mocks the church by using actual historical facts. It is a critical and at times humorous analysis of the church's history from a modern perspective." *Katarina Nolte*

"This was a wild ride. I found parts to be rather upsetting but I think the author really did his homework." *Sher Brown*

"An incredibly clever and humorous take on the Catholic Church." *ChristophFischerBooks*

PAPAL BULL

An Ex-Catholic Calls Out the Catholic Church

ALSO BY JOE WENKE

You Got to Be Kidding! A Radical Satire of The Bible

Mailer's America

Free Air, Poems

The Talk Show, a novel

Looking For Potholes, Poems

*The Human Agenda: Conversations about Sexual Orientation
and Gender Identity*

PAPAL BULL

An Ex-Catholic Calls Out the Catholic Church

JOE WENKE

Stamford, Connecticut

2013

Trans Über LLC
www.transuber.com

Copyright © 2013 by Joe Wenke

All rights reserved under International and Pan-American Copyright Conventions. Published in the United States of America by Trans Über LLC, Stamford, Connecticut.

No part of this book may be reproduced or transmitted in any form or by any means, electronic or mechanical, including photocopy, recording, or any other information storage and retrieval system, except for brief excerpts in a review or essay referring to this book, without prior permission in writing from the publisher.

To reach the author or Trans Über email: josephwenke@msn.com

ISBN: 978-0-9859002-5-0

Digital edition available.

First Edition

Transgender pope: Gisele Alicea (aka Gisele Xtravaganza)
Cover art direction: Gisele Alicea (aka Gisele Xtravaganza)
Book design: Blue Mountain Marketing
Front cover photo: Nina Poon

www.joewenke.org
Follow Joe Wenke on twitter @joewenke.

For Mark, Ryan, Olivia and Gisele

Papal bull: An unintentionally ironic term for a formal pronouncement by a pope.

CONTENTS

Introduction

Growing Up Catholic

What was it like growing up Catholic as a decidedly blue-collar member of the Baby Boom generation of the '50s and '60s? Well, for one thing it was crowded. Almost everybody had big families. I was the oldest of eleven children. We started out in a small rented row home in South Philadelphia and moved in 1958 to another small row home in Glenolden, Delaware County, just a few miles southwest of Philly. My parents bought the house for under $10,000 with a thirty-year mortgage and took the entire thirty years to pay it off. I have no idea how we fit in that house. There was maybe 700 square feet of living space and what I would describe as 2½ bedrooms. The "half bedroom," where I slept with one of my brothers, was a little bigger than a walk-in closet. Six of my siblings slept in two bunk beds in a small middle room. My parents slept in a slightly bigger front room, which somehow accommodated their bed and two cribs. There was one small bathroom.

We never thought of ourselves as poor, but we never had any money. I knew that, so I never asked for anything. When my shoes got holes in them, I used cardboard to cover the holes. When I walked to school on rainy days, the cardboard would get wet. Then my socks would get wet. Then my socks would get holes in them too.

Despite the extremely low price of entry into our neighborhood, which was known as Briarcliffe, there were no black people. For that matter, there were no Hispanic people, no Asian people, and no Jewish people either. I don't think that I met a single person from outside my racial or cultural group until I was eighteen and began working summers at DuPont in West Philly. Everybody I knew was white and Catholic.

My family's move was part of the white flight from Northern industrial cities that marked the late 1950s and '60s. Actually our part of the suburbs was really just another version of South Philly with the addition of little postage stamps of grass and weeds. Nevertheless, the impetus for the move was partly to escape the racial integration of the inner city. If you were black, it was all but impossible to move into our neighborhood. By the early '60s there were maybe a couple of black families who tried to move into neighborhoods within a few miles of where I lived. The adults in my neighborhood referred to them as "blockbusters." Blockbusting was a practice whereby real estate agents frightened white homeowners into selling their homes at a loss with the prospect that their neighborhood was about to become racially integrated. But the term as used by the adults in my neighborhood described the black family that was moving in. They were "blockbusters," the racial integrators and would-be destroyers of the neighborhood who were supposedly backed financially by groups like the NAACP. That at least was the racist myth. Even people who weren't overtly racist believed that black people destroyed the neighborhood once they moved in.

I remember what happened when a black family moved into Folcroft, which was a town maybe three or four miles from where I lived. The house was stoned and vandalized, and the family was driven from the neighborhood in just about no time. It was the summer of 1963. Today there are some black families living in the area where I grew up, but the neighborhoods are still overwhelmingly white, and the economic status of the people living there is about the same, relatively speaking.

So that was the environment—crowded, borderline poor, all white, almost one hundred percent Catholic and racist. Just about everybody went to Catholic school. Public school was out of the question. That was where the black and Protestant kids went.

Talk about crowded! It's hard to say what was more crowded—my house or the school I went to. I started out at St. Monica's in South Philly, but from the second grade on, I went to Our Lady of Fatima. In 1959, the year my sister, Maureen, entered first grade, there were six first grades with about 100 kids in each classroom. Each class was taught by a single nun. At both schools they were the Sister Servants of the Immaculate Heart of Mary. The so-called lay teachers were young women with little or no teaching credentials. My third-grade teacher was an eighteen-year-old woman who had just graduated from high school and was taking evening classes at a local college—I think it was St. Joe's.

Unfortunately all of the clichés about Catholic school in the '50s and '60s are true. School was boring and regimented. There was corporal punishment, too. Today a lot of what went down would rightfully be viewed as physical abuse and in some cases merit arrest. I hated every single second of grade school and high school except for maybe parts of kindergarten and first grade at St. Monica's. Time crept by slowly in those days. It seemed that a century had passed before I graduated from eighth grade.

Amazingly, I remember being kept after school in kindergarten. I was five years old. The class was singing a song, and I was amusing myself by singing like a frog. The teacher, Sister Esperanza, stopped the song and cried out, "Who's singing like that!" I was instantly betrayed. Every kid within an aisle or two of me pointed at me, and I remember batting away their hands and arms from my face as I sank down in my desk. After school the classroom was empty except for me and the sister. She was doing work at her desk at the front of the class. I somehow got it into my head that if I was really quiet and sneaky, I could escape by crawling out of the class on my hands and knees and that she would never know the difference. And so that's what I did. I remember crawling out of the room and then when I got to the hallway running down the stairs and out of the school like a crazy person. The good sister must have had a sense of humor. She must have observed me the whole time, but she let me escape, and I never heard a word from her about the incident the next day at school.

What this little incident also reveals is that at the age of five I did in fact walk by myself to and from school most every day. Imagine anyone letting their kid do that today anywhere in the country let alone through the inner city streets of South Philly. My father worked all day at an oil refinery, and my mother was home at this point with my brother and sister. Before I finished first grade there were two more kids. That's five kids, six years old or younger. So I was pretty much on my own. This meant that my peers and I had a really odd kind of freedom when we weren't in school. We were out of the house all of the time with no adult supervision. In South Philly this meant lots of handball, lots of stickball and lots of fights. I had been in maybe a couple of dozen fights by the time I was seven and we moved.

We almost never told our parents about anything that happened at school no matter how bad it was. I think I did tell my father once about some atrocity that had taken place, and he said something like, "Whatever they did, you must have deserved it."

What did the nuns do? Well, some of them carried around little wooden clickers. They liked to click away on them while they were barking out orders. They also used them as tools for issuing corporal punishment. I remember one time when the nun decided to punish every boy in the class. We had to get in line, march up to her and extend our hands palms down so that she could rap our knuckles with the wooden clicker. That hurt! My brother Jack's first grade teacher would punish the six year olds by putting them in the trash can at the front of the class. Once when I was in seventh grade I got kicked out of the class for talking and laughing. As I closed the door, the wind blew through the classroom, and the door slammed. It was so loud it was like a bomb going off. In two seconds the nun came flying out of the room like a bat out of hell. She grabbed me by the tie, lifted me off the floor and began slapping my face back and forth over and over like she was Moe and I was Curly. The whole time she was slapping me, I was trying to tell her what happened—huffing and puffing in between each slap—"I . . . didn't . . . slam . . . the . . . door . . . it . . . was . . . the wind . . . I . . . didn't . . . do . . . anything!"

The single worst incident I ever saw occurred when I was in eighth grade. Whenever somebody did something wrong, but the nuns didn't know who the guilty party was, they dealt with the situation by punishing every single person in the class. That way they were sure to get the bad guy. I have no idea what the crime was in this particular instance, but I recall that we were all sitting after school in total silence for a really long time. I'm talking about maybe fifty kids sitting after school way past when they were all supposed to be home. Again, just imagine the furor this would cause today. But back then I doubt that anybody's parents even noticed.

I don't know if we were all being loyal to the culprits or whether most of us had no idea what had even happened or who had been involved, but the situation got so extreme that the nun finally decided to bring in the heavy artillery, i.e., the principal of the school, the Mother Superior. While the nun was telling the Mother Superior about whatever crime had been perpetrated and about the entire class's culpability in protecting the identity of the perpetrators, one boy whispered the words, "Sister's a bum." He spoke the words really quietly, but they resonated throughout the entire classroom. Mother Superior heard them clear as a bell. In those days all of the desks were connected on runners, so each row of desks began with a seat without a desk. The Mother Superior ordered the boy to come to the front of the class and lie face down across the seat at the head of the middle row of desks. She picked up one of those thick, heavy yardsticks that every classroom had in those days and proceeded to beat the boy mercilessly. She used both hands on every blow, hitting him as hard as she could each time. She kept it up until the thick yardstick actually broke in two. After that, I think we were all allowed to go home. I guess by then justice had been done. As for the boy, he was expelled from the school. We never saw him again.

I guess you could say that witnessing incidents like that one was an education in its own right. But as far as real education is concerned, I wonder to this day how most of the kids learned much at all. With so many kids, we were really just being warehoused a lot of the time. My worst experience with warehousing came in the fourth and fifth grades. When I was in the fourth grade, the school ran out of classrooms. They decided to take the smartest kids in the fourth and fifth grades and put them together in one room. We were taught half of the day and did "busy work" the other half of the day. Of course, this meant that I was experiencing everything the fourth and fifth grades had to offer at one and the same time, which of course wasn't all that much. But here's the really bad part. The next year they somehow had enough classrooms, and I found myself placed in fifth grade, where I experienced the ineffable pleasure of listening all over again to everything that I had heard the previous year. It didn't help at all when I heard my aunt, who was an Immaculate Heart nun and a teacher in the Philadelphia Catholic schools, tell my father that if I had been in public school, I would have been allowed at some point in my elementary school career to skip a grade.

Whatever we did learn was accomplished mostly through repetition and memorization. Math was called "drill and mental." We memorized multiplication tables, were drilled in long division and were constantly taking quizzes, which were called "mentals." It's probably partly a result of this regimen that I am very good at doing calculations in my head. English was a combination of diagramming sentences, memorizing punctuation rules, learning vocabulary, doing spelling drills and a little reading. Religious instruction was memorizing *The Baltimore Catechism*. At one point I knew the answer to every question in that book. My favorite question and answer combination was "If God is everywhere, why do we not see Him?" "We do not see God, because He is a pure spirit and cannot be seen with bodily eyes." I still think that "bodily eyes" is one of the weirdest phrases anybody has ever come up with.

A number of important subjects got very little attention. We had no science at all, which is just amazing. History and geography were taught using really thin little blue books that you could have read in one sitting. Somehow we never managed to finish the books by the end of the school year. The biggest joke was a subject called "picture study." This was taught using a tiny little book with a handful of photographs of paintings. I remember one of the paintings was Jean-Francois Millet's *The Gleaners*. We would stare at the photograph, while the teacher read from a list of questions about the painting. That was simply thrilling. We never got through the entire picture study book either. Finally, as far as independent thinking was concerned, it just wasn't part of the curriculum.

Of course, the worst part of the whole Catholic experience was the religion itself and all of the emphasis on sin and guilt. It seemed as though we were always in church. You had to go to church every Sunday, of course. Then there were so-called Holy Days of Obligation. You had to go to church on those days, too. New Year's Day was a Holy Day of Obligation. It was originally the feast day of the circumcision of Jesus. That's right. You had to go to church to celebrate the fact that the Son of the Creator of the Universe had the tip of his dick cut off. Maybe even the church decided this was too weird because New Year's Day is still a Holy Day, but now it's to celebrate the "Solemnity of Mary, Mother of God." The Assumption of Mary and the Immaculate Conception are Holy Days, too, and there are a few others as well, including of course, Christmas.

The single worst part of the whole Catholic religion thing was having to go to confession, especially once you hit puberty when you were having sexual thoughts and spontaneous erections nonstop, and you were told that taking even momentary pleasure in any sexual thought was a mortal sin. You were actually supposed to go inside one end of a box and tell a guy sitting in the middle of the box about all sorts of embarrassing personal sexual stuff. That was really a species of abuse in and of itself.

I'm sure just about everybody who grew up in the Catholic Church during the Baby Boom days has stories to tell about going to confession. I certainly have a few. One innocent little story has to do with when the nuns dragged our entire third grade class over to church and forced us to go to confession because we were going to receive the sacrament of confirmation in a couple of days. Confirmation was when you got an additional name—mine is James. Basically it involved the local bishop coming to your church and all of the priests and nuns acting like he was a real big shot. The bishop would give a really long and boring sermon, and then everybody who was getting confirmed had to get in line in order to go and stand in front of him. When you got there, he rubbed some oil on your forehead and tapped you on the cheek and then you sat down. It always seemed to me, and I think to most everybody else, that confirmation was kind of an unnecessary and useless sacrament. I would have certainly gotten rid of it if I had been the pope—speaking infallibly, of course.

Anyway, back when I was eight or nine years old, I probably went to confession about once a month. Coincidentally I had just gone to confession a few days before the nuns forced me to go because of my impending confirmation. When I got into the confession booth, I told the priest that it had been five days since my last confession and that I hadn't done anything wrong. Looking back, I should have just said that very same thing at every single confession I ever made. In any event I was probably in the confession booth for about ten seconds, and when I got back to my pew, I just sat down instead of kneeling and saying my penance. I didn't say my penance because the priest didn't give me any penance to say. Boom! Just like that, the second I sat down the nun came over and wanted to know what was going on. She must have seen me go in and out of the confessional in no time and then just sit down. I looked up at her and said quite sincerely and innocently, "I didn't do anything wrong." She looked at me and just walked away. I realize now that if I had just held on to that one thought—"I didn't do anything wrong"—for the next ten years or so, I would have escaped the whole Catholic guilt trip.

The worst experience I ever had in confession occurred when I was in the eighth grade. At this point I hated going to confession and put it off as long as I could. This particular time I recall that it had been seven weeks since my last confession. Maybe that's a little longer between confessions than the church recommended back in those days but really not that bad when you think of it. Anyway, I had the great misfortune of making this confession to the pastor of Our Lady of Fatima. He was actually the founder of the church, and he was a fucking bastard. He got really bent out of shape that it had been such a long time since my last confession. But you'll never guess how he expressed his righteous anger. He said, "How would you like to go to Darby Township with all the niggers?" Darby Township was the local public school. To this day, I'm astounded by the pathological hatred and racism of that remark. What's more, the good pastor was basically threatening to violate the confidentiality of the confessional and expel me from Our Lady of Fatima all because I hadn't been to confession in seven weeks.

So that's my experience of Baby Boom Catholicism—way too many people, no money, racism, corporal punishment, bad education, boredom and a whole shitload of guilt. The only thing that saved me, and a lot of kids like me, was rock and roll and the Beatles. Hey, because of the weird freedom that we had in those days just by being lost in the crowd, I actually got to see the Beatles at JFK Stadium right at the height of the whole controversy when John Lennon said that the Beatles were more popular than Jesus. I even went to the Electric Factory a few times—I saw Ten Years After open for the Jeff Beck Group with Ron Wood, Nicky Hopkins, Micky Waller and Rod Stewart on vocals. So I got to stand just a few feet away from Alvin Lee and Jeff Beck while they played the blues. Now that's what I call "salvation," and for that experience, all I can do is thank the Lord.

Preface

So that's part of the story of what it was like for me growing up Catholic. Really just a small part of it. Just a few headlines. The whole story would be a book in and of itself. I mean a really big book—bigger than the *Confessions* of St. Augustine, bigger than the *Douay-Rheims Bible*.

The word "pervasive" doesn't begin to describe the influence the Catholic Church had on me, and I know I'm not the only one who's had this experience. There are a whole lot of recovering Catholics walking around in a perpetual state of cosmic rehab. Those of us who are members of this club know that the Catholic Church can truly get to your brain, to the way you look at everything, the way you think and feel about yourself and the world.

If you have OCD, the Catholic Church is definitely the place for you. All you need to do is accept the idea right when you're hitting puberty that having an impure thought is a mortal sin, i.e., that you can be sent to hell for taking momentary pleasure in a sexual thought, and you are set for life. In fact, you will have enough guilt-ridden thoughts to keep you busy not only for the rest of this life but for eternity as well.

When it comes to Catholic guilt trips, I have to say I definitely took the scenic route. Now after all of these years, I still find myself analyzing everything I think and do in moral terms—despite the fact that I think everything is absurd. Now what could be more absurd than that!

For example, I find myself wondering why I wrote this book, and not just this book but the other book that I wrote about religious nonsense called *You Got to Be Kidding! A Radical Satire of The Bible.* As I explain in my Huffington Post piece called "The Genesis of *You Got to Be Kidding!*" which is now the afterword to the book, I woke up one morning, and the first thought that occurred to me was that I would read the Bible and when I found something funny, I would write about it. Now this was really strange because I had never had that thought before, and I don't know why it came to me that day. Also, I don't know why I thought that the Bible was funny, although it is hilarious. Nevertheless, I walked over to my kitchen table in a kind of a trance, sat down at my laptop, immediately downloaded an electronic version of the Bible and started reading. When I came to the Adam and Eve story, I wrote the first sketch of the book. I wrote it really fast as if I were writing an email. Over the next few weeks I read the Bible and wrote more than 70 sketches just the same way, hardly changing a word.

What I didn't say in the article was that as soon as I finished writing *You Got to Be Kidding!* I started writing this book about the Catholic Church. It took me a little longer to write—a few months rather than a few weeks—since I wasn't writing about a single book. I was covering 2,000 years of history, but the experience was pretty much the same. I wrote one piece after another really fast hardly ever changing a word, and before I knew it *Papal Bull* was done.

So what's going on here? Why did this happen? Why did I write these two books?

Well, even though it may seem that I'm begging the question, I think the right answer, the honest answer, is that I had to. I didn't choose to write these books. The books wrote themselves. I can't say that I was inspired by the Holy Spirit. That would be blasphemy, of course, but something weird was definitely going on. Although I always take responsibility for what I do—hello, that's what I was taught to do by the Catholic Church—I think the church has to accept a whole lot of responsibility—and bear a whole lot of guilt—for both of these books as well. I hate pointing fingers, but the truth is the truth. There is no way to escape the fact that growing up Catholic, which I certainly didn't choose—set in motion a very complicated chain of events that eventually led me to writing these two books.

The good thing though is that regardless of why I wrote these books and regardless of who should be blamed for them, they were both great fun to write. In fact, Dear Reader, I hope you have as much fun reading this book (and the other one) as I did writing them. For all those recovering Catholics out there who happen to read my books, I say cheers to you, and I wish you good luck with your never-ending rehab!

BEGINNING AT THE END

OK. You're Dead—Now What?

Nobody knows what happens when you die. But if I were to bet the farm on what happens when you buy the farm, I would say nothing happens. You die and that's it—you're one and done.

If I'm wrong and there is something, the only people who know are dead people, and they're not talking. I don't count whatever voices John Edward and other mediums like him say they're hearing. That nonsense is in the same league as all of those alien sightings in the swamps of Alabama and Mississippi. If there are any aliens in our neighborhood and they want to let us know they're here, they need to land on the White House lawn or maybe in St. Peter's Square. Otherwise, I'm not paying attention. And if any dead person feels the urge to spill the beans about what's going on beyond the grave, if they want to be the first one to break the celestial code of silence, God's omertà, then they should just come right out and broadcast it to the world. Interrupt the flow of atheist comedy on *Real Time with Bill Maher*— just to serve him right—or if they want the biggest possible audience, break up the Super Bowl halftime show. It usually sucks anyway.

Frankly I don't know what purpose it serves to keep the whole afterlife thing so mysterious. I know the Gospel writers have Jesus talk about it, and the Catholic Church and the other churches never stop talking about it, but to be honest, nobody's really satisfied with those explanations—not even the truest of the true believers. I don't know why God doesn't just give us a YouTube video of heaven, hell, purgatory and limbo and put the whole thing to rest. I'll bet it would easily beat all the records for most YouTube views. I'll bet God would just blow away "Gangnam Style," Justin Bieber, "Charlie bit my finger—again!" and everybody else.

On the other hand, if there is nothing, it would be good to know that too—maybe not before you die but how about a split second afterwards? I agree with what George Carlin said about all of this. If there is nothing, it would be great if, when you died, there was a voice that said, "There's nothing," and you got to say "OK" or "fuck" or "Goddamn it" or whatever you chose to say, and then you would be immediately annihilated. That would be cool.

Actually I hope I'm wrong and there is something after you die. Obviously, I don't want to be stuck in a pizza oven (i.e., go to hell), and I don't want to stare at God for eternity, but if I can opt out of the Beatific Vision and just keep on keeping on with a minimum of bother, I'm all for it. Who wants to be annihilated? Not me. But besides that, I really hope that there is a God and an afterlife, because I have a bone or two to pick with the Creator of the Universe, and I'd love to have the chance to pick those bones.

But before I get to the bones I want to pick, there is one other issue that occurs to me if there is a God and there is an afterlife and you do get the chance to meet your maker. And that is—which God shows up? Is it the Old Testament God, the New Testament God, God, the Son— that would be Jesus—or the Holy Spirit? After all, he's God too even though nobody takes him seriously. I mean he does like to show up as a bird most of the time. I sort of think of him as the Fredo of the Trinity.

My preference would be for all of them to show up. Maybe they could just clear their calendars for the meeting. I know they could all gang up on me, and that would be four on one, but then we could get all of the questions out in the open. I mean, if you think about it, it's kind of unfair for any of them to get all judgmental about a puny little human being, like me, in the first place. But I say bring it on. Let's just have it out. I'm dead anyway, so at this point I have to think that I just don't give a shit.

So just for fun, let's pretend they all show up. Here's my first question: Since you are an all-knowing God, you obviously knew before you created the universe and created human beings who was going to heaven and who was going to hell. The Catholic Church says that you have to be baptized to go to heaven. The Catholic Church also says that it is the one true church. Some Catholics actually take this to mean that if you aren't Catholic, you can't go to heaven. Everybody else goes to hell. Others take a more flexible view. Let's not get bogged down in all the differences of opinion here. Let's just say that, however you slice it, tens of billions of people, maybe hundreds of billions of people, have already gone to hell. Depending upon how long human beings continue to live on this planet, we could be talking in the fullness of time about trillions and trillions of people in hell. As I've said elsewhere, maybe the number of people in hell is ultimately googol. I won't even get into the question of whether intelligent life forms on the billions and billions of planets in the universe go to hell, too. In that case we're talking about an extremely serious number of zeros. So let's just say that any way you look at it, there's quite a crowd in hell. My question to God is if you knew this was going to happen ahead of time—why did you create the universe? Why did you create human beings and other intelligent life forms just to end up torturing them all because you didn't like what they believed or how they behaved? I'd like an answer to that question because It seems to me that God's decision to create the universe, knowing that trillions of people and other intelligent life forms were definitely going to hell, is clearly the most despicable act imaginable.

Now I have to admit that if that's my first question, we are off to a pretty rocky start. Any one of the four Gods could take it personally—maybe not Jesus or the Holy Spirit because I don't think they personally take credit for creating the universe, but either the Old Testament God (OTG) or the New Testament God (NTG) could get pretty upset. But as I said, I'm dead, so at this point I'm just letting it all hang out. Besides, I think it would be pretty lame, even for God, to just send me to hell at that point, so I figure no matter what, I'd still have the chance to ask a few more questions.

So here's question number two. It's actually kind of embarrassing, but I just have to ask it. It's basically if you are an all powerful God, then why is the universe such a mess and why do you have so many nasty things in it? I find it very hard to believe that there would be any Black Holes if God actually knew what he was doing when he created the universe. If I were God and I were proud of my creation, I certainly wouldn't have billions of Black Holes sucking up so much of my beautiful universe, sucking it all up like gigantic vacuum cleaners into who knows where. Does that make any sense? No. Also, what's up with all of the natural disasters? Hurricanes, tsunamis, floods, droughts, earthquakes, tornados. I won't list them all. I want an explanation from OTG or NTG why this is all good. I'd also like to know why there are so many nasty ugly things on this earth, like viruses and bacteria and roaches and mosquitoes and bed bugs. I'd really like God to explain exactly how any of these things are good ideas.

Now at this point I'm sure I'm really pissing off at least OTG and NTG. Maybe not Jesus, the kinder, gentler God, and maybe not the Holy Spirit, because I'm thinking that maybe he resents OTG and NTG and would actually like to hear somebody give them a hard time.

If I am wearing out my welcome at this point I would just go to some quick hitting questions, like, why do you like being feared? Why do you want to be worshipped and adored all of the time? I mean it's just so narcissistic. And what about prayer? Why do you always have to be persuaded to do the right thing and help out people who are in trouble? Usually it's your fault that they're in trouble in the first place. If you don't know what I'm talking about just refer to my question about natural disasters. Also, why do you take everything so personally? What's it to you how people think and behave? And why did sending your Son to earth to be murdered make you feel better about all of the bad behavior? That has to be the craziest idea I ever heard of. You're mad at the whole human race because they do stuff you don't like, which you call sin, but you forgive them once you have some of the bad people you're already mad at kill him. Boy, would I like to get some kind of explanation for that insanity! Also, I would love to ask Jesus how he really feels to this day about having been sent on a suicide mission.

OK, so with that last question, I would be done. Now I would assume it would be time for me to be judged. At least that's what the Catholic Church says happens when you die. It's Judgment Day for you. Well, here's another little memo from me to the deity. Who the hell are you to judge me? Nobody has the right to judge me, but least of all God. Did I ask to be born? No. Did I choose my parents? No. Did I select my genes? No. How about my race, ethnicity, country of origin, economic status, sexual orientation, IQ, and the list goes on. I had no control over any of that. Who does? Well, in the scenario we have before us here, a scenario in which there is a God and he created everything—that would be him. So God decides that I'm born and selects all of the critical inputs that make me who I am, and then he judges me for how it all turns out. Once you set all of those inputs, I would say you've pretty much determined how everything is going to turn out. So God wants to judge me when he's the one responsible for me. I should judge him on why he didn't give me a few better breaks.

So I would just tell him, sorry, I'm not interested in being judged. However, I suspect that the result would be pretty much the same as if you told a police officer who was arresting you that you didn't really feel that it was necessary for him to take you to jail. So, assuming I have to be judged, I wonder if I'm entitled to defend myself. I'm sure it's almost impossible under the circumstances to get a defense attorney since I imagine that just about every lawyer gets sent straight to hell. So I would have to defend myself. But I think I have a pretty good defense. Not only did I not choose any of the critical inputs that make me think and behave the way I do, I know that the whole free will thing is just a total crock of shit, and I'm sure God knows it too. I just don't think he's gotten called on this crucial point very often, and he would never bring it up himself. But here's the real scoop: You and I don't consciously decide what we do. Our brains direct all of our thoughts and actions for us before we're aware of what we are doing. I'm sorry, but this is a scientific fact. Check it out. So, speaking for myself, I have to say that my brain is the culprit, not me. It is the one pulling the puppet strings on me, the puppet. So don't blame me, God. Blame my brain, you know, the one you gave me.

We hold people responsible for their actions here on earth to protect individual rights and maintain order in society. All of the people unfortunate enough to have been given criminal brains (by you, God) have to be punished for their crimes and separated from society. But this form of responsibility and punishment makes no sense whatsoever on what I would call the celestial level. I'm betting that even Hitler behaves himself now that he's dead. But even if he doesn't, who cares? What harm can he do? Everybody he's with is already dead.

Free will sounds like a great thing until you realize that it serves as the lynchpin for the whole concept of sin and for all of the guilt trips attached to sin and for all of the horrific punishments that all of the mean and sick holy people hope befall their enemies in the wonderful afterlife. Once you realize that there is no such thing as free will, all of the nonsense about sin and guilt just disappears.

So that's my defense. It's not my fault, God. It's yours. After all, you created everything in the first place—you, not me, not any other human being, are responsible for everything. You're the bad guy.

If this defense doesn't work and God lowers the boom on me, so be it. At least I've had my say. I don't let anybody push me around. Bullies can go fuck themselves. I will always stand up for myself. I do it now while I'm alive, and I'll do it, too, if given the chance, when I'm dead—come hell or high water.

LIMBO

Limbo is my favorite crazy idea in the Catholic Church. Now there are a lot of crazy ideas in the church. Nothing but. The biggest one may be the craziest of all. The Creator of the Universe doesn't like the way people behave. He's really mad about it, so he decides to send his Son to earth to get murdered. Once his Son is executed, he feels a whole lot better about everything and makes up with the human beings that he created in the first place. You really can't top that, but I still like Limbo best.

Limbo may also be the craziest overthink in the history of religion. The logic goes as follows: In order to go to heaven, you have to be baptized. That's because everybody is born in sin, original sin. Every single person forever and ever throughout history is guilty of the sin of Adam and Eve. They disobeyed God by eating a piece of fruit, and we are guilty, too, of that same terrible sin even though we didn't even exist. Baptism somehow eliminates the sin. Baptism involves a priest saying some magical words while he pours water on your forehead. Go figure.

Now Catholic theologians realized that there was a big gap in their thinking about what happened to you after you died. According to the New Testament, you go to heaven if you're good and accept Jesus as your Lord and Savior, or you go to hell, if you're bad. But then they thought, what about unbaptized babies who die before they do anything bad except maybe take a crap in their diapers. That's disgusting,

and there's nothing worse than changing a diaper, but not even the
Catholic Church thinks that a baby should burn in hell forever over a
bowel movement. The only problem is, they can't go to heaven because
of the whole original sin problem and that only goes away when the
priest says the special words and pours water on the baby's head.

To solve this problem, the Catholic Church invented Limbo. After
they thought about it a little more, they actually expanded Limbo into
two sections. There's the section for unbaptized babies, and there's another section for every good person who died before Jesus came down
to earth and died. Before that, God didn't let anybody into heaven,
and so a similar thought process applied. The good people couldn't
be sent to hell, so they had to go to some big holding area until Jesus
died and opened up heaven. If you ask me where the unbaptized babies went who died before Jesus saved everybody, I'll punch you in the
mouth.

Now in the Old Testament everybody just went to Sheol when
they died. That was a big hole in the ground, but apparently that was
wrong, according to the Catholic Church. Now as I point out in my
other book on this nonsense called *You Got to Be Kidding*, if you cal-
culate how many people died before the time of Jesus, you come up
with tens of billions of people—to be precise, you're in the neighborhood of about 46 billion people if we start counting from about 50,000
BC. Now that's a lot of people crammed into a hole, and it's a lot of
people for Limbo to handle too. Don't tell me they're all spirits or souls
and don't take up any room. I don't care. It just seems that once you're
dead the whole idea of privacy is totally gone. If I were one of the unbaptized babies, I would put in a special request to be transferred to
the other Limbo because that place got cleared out with the death of
Jesus. That's assuming they didn't just shut it all down at that point.

Now I don't want to be accused of overthink here either, but I have to say that there was one other point that the smart guys in the Catholic Church actually either didn't think about or they just never talk about it. The Catholic Church believes that human life starts at conception and that at conception you have a soul that distinguishes you as an immortal being and a child of God. That means that a fertilized egg has a soul and is human. That's why Catholics think abortion is murder, even the morning after pill. OK. Here's the problem. A big percentage of fertilized eggs never make it. We're talking around two thirds. They just get flushed out during the mother's next menstrual period or just don't succeed at implanting in the womb. So around twice as many fertilized eggs don't make it compared to those who do. I am quite sure that not a single fertilized egg has ever been baptized. This means that Limbo doesn't just include all of the unbaptized dead babies but all of the unbaptized fertilized eggs that got flushed out in Mommy's period—not to mention billions of unbaptized dead fetuses too.

Overthink. Overthink. Sorry, but this just raises more questions. What state are these unbaptized babies, fetuses and fertilized eggs in for all of eternity? Is somebody going to tell me that since they all have souls that a fertilized egg soul is the same as an adult soul? Are all souls created equal? I mean in every way. For example, is a fertilized egg soul equal to the soul of Einstein, or is he still smarter than everybody else even after he's dead?

Finally, what in the heck is it like to be in Limbo? Is it a big incubator and nursery? Or is everybody just sort of floating around in space? And who takes care of all of these babies, fetuses and eggs? Does heaven send volunteers, maybe a brigade of nannies, nurses and fertility doctors, that spend a month or so in Limbo and then they're relieved by another group? And what does everybody do all day? In heaven you supposedly experience the ineffable joy of the Beatific

Vision—that means staring at God. In Limbo, you're deprived of that. Bummer. So it's either staring at God or nothing. That doesn't sound very interesting. In fact, it must be excruciatingly boring. I don't think I could handle either one for more than about ten minutes. I think I'd just rather be dead.

The Real Story on Purgatory

It's amazing how few people know the real story on purgatory. Even devout Catholics don't know. Not counting me, a non-practicing Atheist, and one of my brothers, who is now a fundamentalist Christian, my family is about as devout a Catholic family as you can get, and they don't know what purgatory is all about. Actually I can't blame them. There's been a kind of soft cover up or institutional denial about the church's teaching on purgatory for decades.

Even in the dark days of the 1950s and early '60s when I was in Catholic school being terrorized by the nuns, I really got a kind of soft and gauzy, kinder, gentler picture of purgatory. At worst it was like being under house arrest or maybe showing up at a pancake house for breakfast and finding out that there were like a million people ahead of you and you probably wouldn't be seated until maybe the middle of the next century. Unfortunately, that is not what purgatory is all about.

If you want to know what purgatory is all about, you need to go to the foremost expert on it. That would be Father F.X. Schouppe, S.J. Father Schouppe wrote the authoritative book on purgatory. It's called *Purgatory: Explained by the Lives and Legends of the Saints.* Fr. Schouppe is also the foremost expert on hell. He's the author of *Hell: Illustrated by Facts Taken from Profane and Sacred History.* (In case you're wondering what "profane" history is it's, uh, well, history. Yes, "profane" history is everything that's ever happened on earth except for what's happened involving Jesus and Mary and the church and the saints and stuff like that; that's what Fr. Schouppe calls "sacred history.") These books were written over a hundred years ago, but don't dismiss them because of that. We're talking eternal truths here, and eternal truths are eternal because they don't ever change. A hundred years is nothing.

How did Fr. Schouppe get to be an expert on purgatory and hell, which would both seem like really difficult subjects to be an expert on since in order to know what's going on in either place, you would think you have to be dead? Well, the answer is simple. Fr. Schouppe just did his homework. He's really like an investigative reporter, and like any good investigative reporter, he doesn't have just one source. In fact, Fr. Schouppe has dozens and dozens of sources and dozens and dozens of testimonials—from whom, you might ask? Well, that's just it. That's what makes Fr. Schouppe's books on purgatory and hell unique. Fr. Schouppe's investigative reporting totally blows the lid off of the lie that nobody ever comes back from the dead. In fact, once he gets past talking about the Catholic Church's doctrine on purgatory and making fun of all of the atheist idiots who don't believe in hell but who are all going to end up there, Fr. Schouppe gets down to telling us the real news: he tells us exactly what it's like on the other side. He does this by reporting in these two books just about every single story of when somebody came back from the dead, appeared to some lucky soul in need of saving, and testified to how horrible purgatory and hell really are.

Let's focus for now on purgatory. I do agree with Fr. Schouppe that it is absolutely essential to know the church's doctrine on purgatory, and as I said, it seems that almost nobody does. So here it is. When you have committed a sin—whether it's, God forbid!—a mortal sin or a venial sin and you make a worthy confession and accept and perform the penance the priest gives you, the sin is forgiven. However, there still remains what the church calls the "temporal punishment" due to the sin. That means that if you die with unrepented venial sins on your soul or are still responsible for the temporal punishment due to your confessed and repented sins, you must suffer in purgatory.

Now the one point on which perhaps Fr. Schouppe goes a bit off track is that he insists that purgatory is an actual place and that it's located next to hell. He admits that, "faith tells us nothing definite regarding the location of Purgatory" but takes the view it is located in a physical place and that that place is "the bowels of the earth." Now we know from reading the Old Testament that Sheol was under the earth. That's where everybody except Elijah went when they died back then because heaven wasn't open yet, and it didn't open up until Jesus came to earth and died for our sins. Elijah was taken to heaven by fiery horses and a fiery chariot about 900 years before heaven officially opened, but he was the only guy there.

Now I have to say that I'll bet you if we were able to drill millions of holes all the way through the earth and come out the other side, we still wouldn't find purgatory or hell down there. They just aren't there. So I think Fr. Schouppe is a little off here, but I'll give him a pass on this because everything else he says about purgatory is exactly in line with the Catholic Church's actual teaching on it. In fact, *The Catholic Encyclopedia* totally backs up Fr. Schouppe on this point, and they cite such doctors of the church as St. Augustine, Pope St. Gregory I (aka Gregory the Great), St. Thomas Aquinas and St. Bonaventure. All of these great Catholic theologians agree that in addition to suffering from separation from God (which is actually the worst pain of all), the souls in purgatory also suffer from burning in a fire. To these great thinkers, Fr. Schouppe adds St. Anselm and St. Bernard. These learned men agree: in purgatory the souls do indeed burn in a fire, and the pain that the souls suffer from the fire and from their separation from

God is greater than any pain that anyone could possibly experience on earth. Indeed, Fr. Schouppe also draws heavily upon the knowledge of the saints received through "supernatural communication." Quoting St. Catherine of Genoa, Fr. Schouppe informs us that, "no tongue can express, no mind form any idea of what Purgatory is. As to the suffering it is equal to that of Hell."

So the suffering that you experience in purgatory is really the same as the suffering you would experience in hell—no vision of God and burning in a pizza oven—with the major exception that you know you will some day be released. You just don't know when. It could be in the next instant or it could be billions and billions of years in the future—maybe even billions and billions of years after the universe ceases to exist—so far into the future that it is barely even imaginable. After all, eternity is a really long time.

Now as I said, Fr. Schouppe provides countless testimonials from dead people confirming the Catholic doctrine on purgatory. You really need to read his book to get the full monty on this. But I'll provide a few examples to give you an idea.

First, let me emphasize by quoting Fr. Schouppe that the appearances he describes of the dead are "objective phenomena." Indeed, he states that the appearance of the dead "to the living is a fact that cannot be denied." Fr. Schouppe goes even further. Based on the testimony of Venerable Bede, he relates the story of a good Christian family man from Northumberland named Drithelm, who after dying and receiving a guided tour of the horrors of purgatory, actually rose from the dead. His testimony adds a new dimension to our knowledge of purgatory. He relates that in addition to the fire, there are also ice and snow. When the torment of the fire becomes unbearable—and I would suppose that this would be after maybe one nanosecond—the poor suffering souls run over to the ice and snow and jump in, and then when this torture becomes too great, they jump back into the flames.

God sent Drithelm back to life to bear witness to these horrible truths of purgatory. When he rose from the dead, even though he had previously led an exemplary life, he announced to his family that he would now live quite differently. He divided up most of his possessions among his wife and children, gave whatever was left to the poor so that he had absolutely nothing, went to a nearby abbey and begged to be allowed to stay as a servant to the monks. He was given a cell by himself, where he lived the rest of his life preparing himself for death. Drithelm strongly recommends that we all live this way. We should all live every minute of our lives preparing for death. Indeed, the rest of his life was devoted to just three activities—"prayer, the hardest labor and extraordinary penances." For example, as Fr. Schouppe relates, "in winter he was seen to plunge himself into frozen water, and remain there for hours and hours in prayer, whilst he recited the whole Psalter of David." Clearly, when God allowed Drithelm to return to life, he also granted him the extraordinary power—even beyond what we know of someone like the great Harry Houdini—to hold his breath for a virtually unlimited amount of time. He also must have been given him a special waterproof Book of Psalms, but I suppose once you've risen from the dead, almost anything is possible.

Similarly Fr. Schouppe relates the incredible story of the great virgin, St. Christine the Admirable (aka St. Christina Mirabilis and St. Christina the Astonishing). Christine rose from the dead in very dramatic fashion: at her funeral while everyone was gathered to mourn her death, she sat up in her coffin and began telling everybody about the horrors of purgatory and hell. While she was dead, she actually had a conversation with God himself, who gave her the choice of staying dead and going to heaven or coming back to earth and spending the rest of her life suffering excruciating pain to help relieve the suffering of the souls in purgatory and to provide an example of how we all should live. Of course, Christine chose to return to life on earth and spent the rest of her life in self-imposed deprivation and suffering of the most extreme kind. Indeed, she lived without shelter or any means of support and sought out every conceivable means of torturing herself. For example, she would jump into a furnace and stay in the fire for the longest time, letting out blood curdling screams. When she finally emerged from the fire, she would not be burned at all. On the other hand, in the winter, rather like Drithelm but with even more extraordinary breath control, she would plunge into an icy river and stay there not for minutes or hours or days but actually for weeks at a time.

Although the resurrected lives of Drithelm and St. Christine the Admirable may provide examples of superhuman degrees of deprivation and suffering that none of us could possibly emulate, they do illustrate that the most devout path in life is to prepare constantly for death and that suffering and self-deprivation are redemptive, benefiting the souls in purgatory and purifying our own souls so that we can reduce or even entirely avoid spending any time there when we die.

So we realize that the dead have come back in visitations and even in the flesh to provide us with their first-hand knowledge and experience of purgatory. But the visitations actually work both ways. Fr. Schouppe points out that St. Catherine de Ricci visited purgatory every Sunday night. St. Lidwina of Schiedam and Blessed Osanna of Mantua visited too, accompanied by angels. St. Frances of Rome also received a guided tour of both purgatory and hell.

If you consider yourself a Roman Catholic and don't believe in the Catholic doctrine on purgatory, maybe you should reconsider which religion you really belong in. I'm not saying love it or leave it. I'm not like that. I just mean that maybe instead of being a Catholic you're really an Episcopalian or a Unitarian or a nondenominational liberal Christian, and you just don't know it. I always think it's better to know the truth and act accordingly than to continue living in self-delusion.

HELL

Hell continues to be very popular. It's one of the most cherished beliefs of so many people. I can't prove it, but I bet a lot of people love hell even more than they love Jesus. After all, what's better than the idea of absolute, final judgment being carried out against people you hate? The answer is nothing.

Go to hell! It just feels so goddamn good to say that, doesn't it, especially if you actually believe that hell exists.

The funny thing is that a lot of people who believe in hell are absolutely certain that almost everybody is going to hell—just not them. They believe that everybody who is different from them—everybody from a different religion, race, ethic background, nationality, sexual orientation, economic status, political persuasion—are all going to hell. Even people who are just like them in so many ways, but they hate for one reason or another—those people are all going to hell too. These good, God-fearing people just seem to like the idea of living forever in a seriously under-populated heaven with plenty of room for them to move around.

The idea of an all-loving, all-knowing God who sends to hell, who condemns to never ending torture in an inextinguishable fire, just about everybody he creates, is one of the funniest things imaginable. It's really the biggest joke of all time because it shows almost better than anything else how stupid we human beings are. Suppose God did send just about everybody to hell and somehow you were one of the lucky ones who didn't go there, why would you want to hang out with that motherfucker? Wouldn't that be like having dinner with Hitler instead of being shoved into an oven at Auschwitz? Instead of being dragged off to a concentration camp, you got a dinner invitation from the Fuhrer, and you checked your calendar to see if you had a conflict. Hey, I would tear up that fucking dinner invitation. Or maybe I would just RSVP my regrets to Adolf—same with hanging out in heaven with a God who sends almost everybody else to hell. I would opt out. I would rather just go to hell. Actually I would wish that I had just never been born.

So what about hell? Well, we can of course turn to our expert, Fr. Schouppe, but we don't really need him that much for hell. We all pretty much know about hell. Besides, Fr. Schouppe's hell book is really not on the same grand, dare I say epic, level as his tome on purgatory. First of all, Fr. Schouppe's *Hell* is really more of a monograph than a book. Also, Fr. Schouppe gets off to a rather rocky start. Right off the bat, he betrays a very disturbing attitude toward everybody who is not a Roman Catholic, not a believer in the one, true faith. Asserting the almost universal belief in hell through the ages, he says, "Hell has never been denied by heretics, Jews or Mohammedans." Ouch! Fr. Schouppe, that is really nasty. That's like saying even the scum of the earth believe in hell. He then adopts a gloating, almost giddy, tone toward all of the atheists—hey, that's me, even though I'm nonpracticing—who don't believe in hell but are going to end up there some day.

That's pretty bad. That's just plain juvenile. But you know what? I forgive you, Fr. Schouppe. You probably just couldn't help it. I forgive you wherever you are right now, which is probably nowhere. I'll probably be nowhere really soon, and so will everybody else. So I forgive you. After all, that's just the way your brain worked, Fr. Schouppe. It was your brain talking, not you, so I can't really blame you.

Of course, we can always count on Fr. Schouppe to provide us with some really incredible stories that you just won't find anywhere else. In his purgatory book he tells countless stories of people who came back from the dead to tell us how bad purgatory is and how we should all change our lives and suffer and practice self-denial and live with a constant focus on death. In *Hell* he provides the same valuable service, telling one story after another of people who died, were condemned to hell and were sent back to earth briefly by an all-just, all-merciful God to give all of us poor sinners a truly horrifying view of the unspeakable torment that awaits us all if we don't repent.

As I mentioned, Fr. Schouppe has tons and tons of stories of people returning from the dead, but I'll give just a couple of examples. A sixteen-year-old servant girl in Peru by the name of Martha became gravely ill. The priest came and she made her confession, but afterward she told her servant girl friends that she had concealed some of her sins from the priest. Her friends got really upset and told the mistress of the house, who immediately brought back the priest and made Martha confess her sins all over again. Shortly after confessing a second time, Martha died. When she died, a terrible stench immediately filled the room, and her body had to be moved to a shed in the backyard. A dog who stayed back there and who was normally quiet and well behaved began moaning and howling horribly.

After Martha was buried, strange things started happening. A big stone fell out of the sky and landed on the patio table right in front of the lady of the house. That night all of the furniture in Martha's room began flying around, and the room shook as if there were an earthquake. Then Martha herself appeared to her servant friends. She was in a horrible state, totally engulfed in flames. According to Fr. Schouppe, she told her friends that she had been condemned to hell "for her sins of impurity and for the sacrilegious confessions she had continued to make until her death."

As one might expect, Fr. Schouppe also relates the stories of people who lived what he calls "dissipated" lives given to wine, women and song. In addition, he tells several stories of people who seemed to live good, Christian lives but were maybe a little vain or immodest in dress. In fact, we learn that "a noble lady" once prayed for God to reveal to her what "displeased his Divine Majesty most in persons of her sex." The good Lord blessed her with a vision of one of her deceased friends suffering unspeakable tortures in hell. Her unfortunate friend told her that during her life she had taken "to adopt indecent fashions to attract attention" and "had kindled the fire of impurity in more than one heart."

Notwithstanding the unbelievable testimony of that last vision, I still have to say that it really doesn't seem that the people Fr. Schouppe talks about here—the people who are condemned to hell—are really all that bad. I mean what did they do to deserve being tortured forever in a fire? That's obviously a worse punishment than getting the death penalty, which almost every civilized country except the United States has abolished and which is only reserved for the most horrific crimes. But here are people who maybe liked to fuck around or drink a little bit or dress a little bit sexy, or maybe they were just too embarrassed to tell a priest some really personal things about themselves, and for these high crimes they are damned forever.

Actually that's what I was brought up to believe. Back in those dark days of the 1950s and '60s it seemed like just about everything was a mortal sin. You could go to hell for having an impure thought, missing Mass on Sunday, not going to communion or confession during Easter time, or eating meat on Friday. It was just so easy back then to commit a mortal sin. To illustrate, let's imagine that a little boy named Joey woke up late for school one day. Maybe his mother over-slept or he overslept—whatever. Joey is late for school, he's running around trying to get ready as fast as he can, his mother is running around too. Joey throws his clothes on really quickly, his mother makes his lunch as fast as she can, and Joey is so late that he doesn't even eat breakfast. So now Joey is at school, it's lunchtime, and he's just starving to death. He opens up his little brown lunch bag, and what does he find? It's a big, fat baloney sandwich. Oh, no! Today is Friday, and in all of the hubbub and uproar over being late for school, Joey's mother forgot that it was Friday and that you just can't eat a baloney sandwich on Friday. Joey knows it's Friday. He knows it's a mortal sin to eat the baloney sandwich, but he's starving, so he eats it anyway.

The baloney sandwich revives Joey, and he's all excited to go out-side and play in the schoolyard with his friends, so he runs out of the classroom and into the driveway without looking where he's going, and—bam! Just like that the pastor, Father Gaffney, runs Joey over in his big black Cadillac. Joey is killed instantly and is immediately dragged away by demons to everlasting torture in hell.

I always wonder about all of the baloney lovers in hell. It's not a mortal sin any longer, in fact it's no sin at all, to eat meat on Friday (except during Lent—then it's still a mortal sin). You can even com-pete in a hot dog eating contest on Friday now, and it's perfectly fine with the Catholic Church. I really hope that God reconsidered and released all of the Friday meat eaters from hell and at least let them graduate to purgatory, where they would still be tortured by an inex-tinguishable fire and suffer worse pain than you can ever experience here on earth. I hope that maybe after another billion years when the earth gets swallowed up by the sun, the good Lord would let all of those poor meat eaters, like our poor unfortunate little Joey, into heaven. I hope that's the case, but I doubt it. I just don't think that's the way God rolls.

Now if you think all of this stuff about how almost every little thing is a mortal sin is from the Dark Ages and that the church is a lot more progressive now, think again. I found a "Mortal Sin Check-Off List" put together apparently by a devout Catholic, a person who would seem to be exactly like the people I described at the beginning of this little piece—a person who is clearly in love with the idea of hell and believes that most people are gong there, but definitely not him. In fairness the checklist is intended to be helpful. It's to help you make a thorough examination of conscience before you go to confession to make sure that you don't forget or overlook a single mortal sin. I mean it would be pretty easy to do that because so very many things are, as the checklist suggests, "possible/probable mortal sins." Here is a brief sample of "possible/probable mortal sins":

- Did you put your faith in Astrology?

- Did you put your faith in Eastern Philosophies?

- Did you put your faith in Atheism? (Say, what?)

- Did you join, contribute to, or sympathize with Planned Parenthood?

- Did you join, contribute to, or sympathize with the ACLU?

- Did you join, contribute to, or sympathize with Gay Rights Groups?

- Did you join, contribute to, or sympathize with Pro-Choice Groups?

- Did you join, contribute to, or sympathize with the Communist Party?

- Did you join, contribute to, or sympathize with the Socialist Party?

- Were you married by a Justice of the Peace (without Dispensation)?

- Did you use God's name as a curse?

- Did you fail to eat properly, and become anorexic, through Vanity?

- Did you take or sell Illegal Drugs?

- Did you Abuse Alcohol (Willful Drunkenness)?

- Do you have excessive Body Piercings?

- Do you have a piercing of the nipples or sexual organs?

- Did you commit Fornication (sex before marriage)?

- Have you engaged in, promoted, or used Prostitution?

- Have you viewed Pornography?

- Do you have a sexual Fetish?

- Did you have impure or violent sexual fantasies, asleep or awake?

- Have you watched Impure Television, Movies, or DVDs?

- Have you kissed or touched another to cause Arousal, who's not your spouse?

- Have you caused sexual climax, without Intercourse, even with your spouse?

- Did you commit Onanism (withdrawal for Contraceptive purposes)?

- Did you have Oral Sex (except for Married Partners—Oral foreplay is OK ONLY IF ejaculation is vaginal)?

- Did you Masturbate?

- Did you engage in Homosexual Acts?

- Did you have Anal Sex, or other degrading sexual practices?

- Did you use a contraceptive device (condom, diaphragm, intrauterine device)?

- Did you practice the Rhythm Method of birth control, even with your spouse?

- Did you engage in In-Vitro Fertilization?

- Did you engage in Artificial Insemination?

- Did you engage in Surrogate Motherhood?

- Did you Cohabit (live together) before Marriage?

- Are you guilty of Transvestitism (Cross Dressing)?

- Did you love sex (or food, etc.) excessively?

- Have you padded your Expense or Per Diem account?

- Have you Pirated computer software or bootlegged movies or DVDs?

- Have you Evaded or cheated on your Tax Return?

I apologize for the length of the list. I can only say in my defense that I left out more than three-quarters of the "Possible/Probable Mortal Sins." I apologize too for the Cotton Mather-like use of capitalization, although it was good to see "Anal Sex" capitalized. I have to admit that even I didn't know that you could commit a mortal sin while you were asleep, but apparently you can if you have "an impure or violent sexual" dream. Also, I thought the Catholic Church was OK with using the rhythm method, especially since it doesn't work. Finally, the next time you decide to put a check in the mail for Planned Parenthood and you're thinking it's such a nice day, you'll just take a little walk and mail your letter at the Post Office, make sure you look both ways before crossing any streets.

Postscript to Hell: Our friend who so kindly put together the "Checklist of Possible/Probable Mortal Sins," has also provided us with a "Checklist of Venial Sins and Other Imperfections." Interestingly, he includes "failure to believe in hell" and "failure to accept that our Most Merciful God allows most people to go to hell" as venial sins or imperfections. Here are a few more that you should watch out for:

- Playing Dungeons and Dragons, (or similar games)

- Being embarrassed at being a Catholic

- Disparaged the church because of the recent sex scandals and cover- up

- When voting, fail to consider the Moral standings of politicians

- Failure to evangelize

- Attended a Catholic/non-Catholic Wedding in a non-approved setting

- Attended the Wedding for a Divorcee before the death of the first spouse

- Failure to bow, remove your hat, or Bless Yourself, etc., when passing a church

- Telling Irreverent Jokes about Sacred Persons, or Objects

- Hired others for the care of your children without good cause

- Had your wife unnecessarily take employment away from home, and children

- Preference for Designer Label Clothes

- Listening to Bad Music

- Excessive Watching of Television

- Excessive playing of Computer Games

- Excessive use of the Internet

- Being Too Strict with Rules, Boundaries, and Discipline

- Being Too Lax with Rules, Boundaries, and Discipline

- Overcapitalization (actually I added that)

Heaven

Any way you look at it, there's really not much to recommend heaven. If there is a hell and God sends almost everybody there and for some reason, he lets me into heaven even though I didn't believe in him and thought that he was a fucking asshole, I wouldn't go precisely because he would indeed have proven himself to be the fucking asshole that I thought he was. It would sort of be like being a Conscientious Objector back in the Vietnam War days. If there is no hell or purgatory for that matter and heaven is the Beatific Vision, then I'm sorry, but I have absolutely no interest in that either. I find the sheer cosmic narcissism of the BV to be totally disgusting. I know a couple of narcissists, and they are the two biggest assholes that I know or can even imagine this side of the deity. So either way, I'm going to say thanks, but no thanks, to heaven.

Even if the Beatific Vision were to give me a huge spiritual hard on, I still couldn't get into it because I know from all of the Viagra and Cialis commercials that if you have an erection for more than four hours, you either need to seek immediate medical help or go to the video tape and upload footage of your amazing erection to YouTube. I would think that an erection lasting for all of eternity would be extremely uncomfortable, not to say unsightly and embarrassing as well.

Most people want to go heaven because it means they didn't go to hell, or else they want to go to heaven because they've decided that heaven will be whatever they want it to be—like they'll be reunited with all of their loved ones and live happily ever after and so on and so forth. For example, if they want to see their kids as kids instead of how they looked when they died in old age—like maybe all broken down and sick and nasty, then they can see them that way. Similarly if their kids want to see their parents the way they remember them when their parents were young and they were kids, they can do that too. That would be nice. Of course, none of this fairy tale stuff is based on anything except really crazy wishful, delusional thinking.

I also wonder about what the rules might be in heaven. Like what you can and can't do. For example, is the Bill of Rights still in effect? Is there freedom of speech? What about freedom of religion? Suppose I'm staring right at God, and I say to him, I don't believe in you any way. What happens? I would assume there's no right to bear arms because it would just be totally unnecessary. I mean if you shot somebody, how would that help? Everybody's dead anyway.

When you read my chapter on the resurrection of the body, you'll see that I do have a big problem with the whole "End of Days" party idea, but maybe having some kind of heavenly body is our best hope. Yes, it would be extremely crowded, and that would be very annoying, but if you at least have your body you can still fuck and beat off and also maybe do some of the things in heaven that you liked doing when you were alive—like go out to eat or maybe just sit by yourself and drink a bottle of wine every night.

Now don't get me wrong. I'm not trying to duplicate the whole wishful thinking, delusional thinking fallacy, I'm really just trying to figure out how this whole heaven idea could possibly work, and I guess if given a choice of having a body or not having a body, I'd go with having a body.

The idea of being a spirit and zipping around the universe at least as fast as the speed of light may sound pretty cool, but after awhile

I think it would get to be a "been there, done that" type of situation and all that would be left is floating in space and casting an occasional glance, if you could stand it, at the cosmically boring BV.

So I guess I'm just not a big fan of the idea of heaven. When you get right down to it, it doesn't sound that much better than being on life support. So maybe it would be best if God just pulled the plug. If I'm missing something here and anybody out there has some good ideas on how heaven might actually be better than just being dead, tweet me @joewenke. I'd love to know.

Them Bones

The Catholic Church has a thing about bones, specifically the bones of saints, which it calls "relics." The church believes that the bones and body parts of saints as well as their clothing and items they have touched or have touched their bones, body parts or even their tombs should be venerated because they have been bestowed by God with special powers. The idea is basically that veneration of relics can secure on behalf of the believer the intercession of the saint with God.

As charitable as one might strive to be, it is rather difficult to view the veneration of a saint's jaw or leg or heart as anything but a gross and rather ghoulish superstition. You pay your respects and give honor to the blessed bones in the belief that the saint who left said bones behind will put in a good word for you with the deity.

Not surprisingly, the veneration of relics has encouraged countless fraudulent claims. Numerous churches throughout Europe have claimed to possess splinters of wood from the "true cross." A number of churches have even claimed to have had the "Holy Prepuce," which I am embarrassed to report is supposedly the foreskin of Jesus. Unfortunately, I believe that the Holy Prepuce has since gone missing. The so-called "Aachen relics" include the dress Mary wore when she gave birth to Jesus, Jesus' swaddling clothes, the loincloth Jesus wore when he was crucified and a towel that was wrapped around the head of John the Baptist—I'm assuming after his beheading. Relics of Jesus are much easier to find than you might expect. In various locations around the world, you can find wood from the manger where he was born, the bench he sat on at the Last Supper, the chalice he used at the Last Supper, the staircase from the palace of Pontius Pilate, the pillar that Jesus was tied to, the cloth that Veronica used to wipe his face during the crucifixion, his robe, the crown of thorns, the nails used in his crucifixion, the spear that pierced his side, the sponge that was soaked in vinegar, and a reliquary that holds several drops of his blood (I assume they've dried by now.). The most famous relic of Jesus is of course the "Shroud of Turin," which is a burial cloth that is purported to bear the image of Jesus.

Relics are by no means rare. In fact, the church has established a practice whereby relics are supposed to be placed beneath every altar in every church. Many churches place their relics on display. Here is a brief list of where you can find some notable relics:

- Bodies of some of the baby boys supposedly killed by King Herod at the time of Jesus' birth are located in five different churches: the Roman basilicas of St. Paul Outside the Walls and St. Mary Major, the Church of St. Justina in Padua and the cathedrals of Lisbon and Milan.

- The bones of the Wise Men who brought gold, frankincense and myrrh to the Baby Jesus are in a gigantic reliquary in the Cathedral of Cologne, Germany.

- Mary Magdalene's femur and some of her hair are in a cave that has been converted into a church in Provence, France.

- St. Simeon Stylites' right hand is in a hand-shaped reliquary at the Monastery of the Transfiguration of the Savior in Beroea, Greece; a fragment of the pillar that he stood on for 37 years is in a ruined church that bears his name in Aleppo, Syria.

- St. Patrick's lower jaw is in the Church of St. Colman and St. Patrick in Derriaghy, Ireland.

- The tongue of St. Anthony of Padua is on display at the Basilica of Il Santo in Padua, Italy.

- One of St. Teresa of Avila's fingers, a board she used for a pillow and a cord she used to flagellate herself are on display at the Convent of St. Teresa; her heart and one of her arms are in the Carmelite convent at Alba de Tormes in Spain.

- The skull and hands of St. Blaise are in the Church of St. Blaise in Dubrovnik, Croatia.

- The head of St. Catherine of Siena, attired in a Dominican nun's headdress, is displayed in the Church of St. Dominic in Siena; one of her feet is in the Church of Sts. John and Paul in Venice.

- The heart of St. Charles Borremeo is in an altar of the Church of Sts. Ambrose and Charles in Rome.

- St. Francis De Sales' heart is in the Monastery of the Visitation in Treviso, Italy.

- A bone from one of the fingers of St. Louis (King Louis IX) is in the Basilica of St. Denis outside of Paris.

- One of Blessed Edward Oldcorne's eyes is at Stonyhurst College in Lancashire, England.

- The humerus bone of St. Frances Xavier Cabrini's right arm is in the Shrine Church of Our Lady of Pompeii in Chicago.

- At one time or another five different churches have claimed to have the skull of St. George.

- The blood of St. Januarius is kept in a vial at the Cathedral of St. Januarius in Naples. The vial of 1,700-year-old blood supposedly liquefies when it is publicly displayed on three different feast days each year. Actually sometimes it liquefies, and sometimes it doesn't. The faithful think that when the blood doesn't liquefy that maybe Januarius is displeased.

- In the Church of St. Ursula in Cologne, Germany, there is an elaborate arrangement of bones covering the walls and ceiling. These are displayed as the bones of St. Ursula and some of the 11,000 virgins. Apparently the Church of St. Ursula has decided to continue to ignore the memo that St. Ursula and her 11,000 virgins never existed.

Now those are some pretty attractive relics that I just described, so maybe you're thinking that you sort of like the whole idea of relics and you might want to acquire some relics of your own, maybe start your own collection. Well, I'm afraid that I must in good conscience tell you that the church strictly forbids the sale of relics. That's called simony, and it's a really bad sin. But if that doesn't faze you, because you're thinking, hey, I would be the buyer, not the seller, you can buy relics on eBay any time you want. At the time this was written there were almost 3,500 items on sale. They included a reliquary containing wood from the true cross, a bandage St. Padre Pio used to cover his stigmata and a real treasure trove: a reliquary containing some hair and mother's milk from Mary, the Mother of Jesus, as well as her veil along with the relics of 21 saints. Prices ranged from just a few dollars into the thousands. The Padre Pio bandage was listing at $3,000.

Incorrupt Bodies

In addition to venerating the bones of dead saints, the church also puts the dead bodies of saints on display. In some instances it claims that the saints' corpses are incorrupt, i.e., have not decomposed. Supposedly if you are really holy when you die, God sometimes decides to override the laws of physics and biochemistry and keep your body intact. In a few instances he even makes your body smell really good like maybe you had just sprayed on some Givenchy Angels and Demons and would be all set to go out on the town for the evening if it weren't for the fact that you were dead. This is called the "odor of sanctity." Too bad the guy who came up with that phrase couldn't think of a better word than "odor."

Supposedly when St. Teresa of Avila died, the entire monastery was filled with a wonderful, heavenly fragrance, as if she had just set off a celestial air freshener at the moment of her death. It smelled really good too when St. Therese de Lisieux, the Little Flower, died. It was like roses, actually, and the fragrance lasted for days.

Some of the incorrupt corpses on display do look pretty good at first glance like St. Bernadette Soubiros, but in reality Bernadette doesn't look any better than the wax figures at Madame Tussauds. In fact, her face and hands are covered by wax masks.

The incorrupt corpses are undoubtedly a big tourist attraction for churches and monasteries around the world. But it may not always be such a positive experience for the tourists. I know I'd be upset if I saw an incorrupt dead body, and it was looking healthier and more attractive than me. For example, in 2000 when Blessed Pope Pius IX was dug up 122 years after he died, he was said to be in great shape and still smiling. Apparently death just agrees with some people.

THE RESURRECTION OF THE BODY

I really don't want to be around for this, but apparently I have to be. Catholics believe that when the world ends, Jesus returns and the dead come back to life. Yes, amazingly that's what they believe. When the world finally comes to an end, there will be zombies everywhere. When I say everywhere, I mean everywhere.

Now I have to say that I am a little confused on what is meant by "the world." Is the world just this little, tiny insignificant planet, or is the world the universe? If the world is just this little, tiny insignificant planet and it ends and Jesus comes back, does everybody on the hundreds of billions of other planets with intelligent life, just keep on going? Or are they having their own "End of Days" parties as well? I just don't know. I'll bet nobody does, not even the pope.

Let's just say that we're only talking about the earth, and we just don't care what's happening anywhere else. That's pretty much our attitude anyway. That's how we roll. We're totally invested in out of sight, out of mind. But given that, what would it be like to experience the "End of the World" here on earth?

Well, if the world ended right now, I would be left holding two unused tickets to see *The Book of Mormon*, which would be a shame, but as Jesus says, "you know neither the day nor the hour," so let's say the day is today, and the hour is 10:00 p.m. eastern time right as the Rachel Maddow Show is ending, along with Pierce Morgan and Sean Hannity. Anyway, if the world ended then you would have by the best estimates I've seen about 108 billion zombies suddenly on the prowl. That's the result of a little more than 50,000 years of procreation. When you think about it, it's really a shame that there aren't a whole lot more gay people fucking away without procreating or a lot more people diligently practicing birth control. If there were, we'd be in a lot better shape when the world ends. I mean it just wouldn't be so goddamn crowded.

That's if the world ended today. Suppose we went another 50,000 years. Well, then obviously if we procreated at roughly the same rate, there would be twice as many zombies or a total of 216 billion.

If we really want to get crazy about this, suppose Jesus just said, fuck it, I'm not lifting a finger to end the world. I'll just let the sun do all the work for me. Well, then we would have maybe a billion more years. Right, a billion. The sun will take about 7.6 billion years to finally die out, but its expansion into a red giant would get us long before then since that process will evaporate the oceans and turn the earth into a desert before the sun itself finally engulfs the planet. This of course does not take into account all of the possibilities for the people on earth figuring out some technological solution to survive the death of the sun—whether that's moving to another planet or changing the orbit of the earth or whatever.

But let's imagine that we did have another billion years. How many zombies would there be showing up for the big Second Coming event? OMG! If procreation continued at the current rate, that would be about two million one hundred eighty thousand billion zombies here on earth. That is pretty frightening because it would make the earth even more crowded than the house I grew up in, and I just couldn't handle that a second time. I would rather be dead, but here's the really bad thing: I would be dead, but it would all be happening anyway.

Anybody out there who really thinks prayer works, I beg you to get Jesus to change his mind about the resurrection of the body. I'm telling you, it will be the biggest mess that anybody has ever seen. The only way I'm changing my mind is if having a body means you can fuck in heaven.

BACK TO THE BEGINNING

WHO STARTED THE CATHOLIC CHURCH?

Did Jesus start the Catholic Church? The Catholic Church says that he did. I wonder what he would say about that.

Jesus was a man—and God—if you believe what he says about himself in the Gospels. But he wasn't a church. Maybe he wanted to start a church. I don't know, but that's different. In Matthew's Gospel (16: 15-19), Jesus asks the disciples the big question: "Who do you say that I am?" Simon Peter says, "'you are the Christ, the Son of the living God.'" Jesus is really happy with that answer. He says, "'blessed are you, Simon Bar-Jonah! For flesh and blood has not revealed this to you, but my Father who is in heaven. And I tell you, you are Peter, and on this rock I will build my church, and the gates of hell shall not prevail against it. I will give you the keys of the kingdom of heaven, and whatever you bind on earth shall be bound in heaven, and whatever you loose on earth shall be loosed in heaven.'"

Now this is a really important passage. It's meaning has been debated by Catholics and Protestants for centuries. The funny thing is Matthew is the only Gospel writer who reports that Jesus said all of this stuff. In Mark (8:29) and Luke (9:20), Jesus does ask the disciples the same question: "Who do you say that I am?" And Simon Peter gives a similar, though not the same, answer. In Mark, he says, "You are the Christ." and in Luke, he says, "the Christ of God," but Jesus doesn't get all excited in either of these accounts and declare that Peter is the rock on which he'll build his church, and he doesn't give him the keys of the kingdom of heaven. You really have to wonder why Mark and Luke leave out all of the important stuff about Peter. Did they leave it out, or did they just have a really bad editor? You also have to wonder why John doesn't mention this scene at all. Did he never write about this scene, or was his account somehow left on the cutting room floor?

These questions don't seem to bother most people. They certainly don't bother centuries of Catholics and Protestants who debate the meaning of the passage from Matthew. Catholics think that the passage means that Jesus is transferring his authority to Peter and is making him the leader of his church. In essence, he's naming him the first pope, and he's saying that all future popes have the same authority as well. This interpretation is the basis for the Catholic Church stating that it is the one true church and that it was founded by Jesus.

Protestants say that's all wrong. They say that Jesus is basing his church on the faith expressed by Peter when he says, "you are the Christ, the Son of the living God," not on Peter himself or anybody else. They say that Jesus is not making Peter the leader of his church. He is not making him a pope. In fact, they say Jesus never said that he wanted popes. They say that popes are a big part of the problem with the Catholic Church.

The dispute over papal authority was a powerful catalyst for the Protestant Reformation. Of course, when the reformers broke away from the Catholic Church, they created their own denominations or brands of Christianity—most of them saying that they were now the ones with the corner on the truth.

Wow! How do you base the authority for a religion or the institution of a religion on correctly parsing the meaning of a single remark? In this case, the all-important statement isn't even recorded by three of the four guys who provide us with the only information we have about

Jesus (I'm not counting the apocryphal Gospels that didn't make the cut and failed to get into the Bible). Even if the exact statement in Matthew 16 were found in the other three Gospels, it isn't at all clear what Jesus is saying.

Of course, quoting the Gospels simply begs the real question: what do we actually know about Jesus? There is no definitive dating of the Gospels, and the earliest complete manuscripts are actually from the fourth century. However, they were certainly written decades after the events they describe. The earliest date that is accepted, even traditionally, for any of the Gospels would place the Gospels of Mark and Matthew as having been written in the '50s C.E., although the scholarly consensus now places their authorship a decade or more later. The consensus for Luke is in the '80s, while the consensus for John is from the '90s to as late as 110. Jesus is believed to have died in the early to mid '30s.

Whoever wrote the Gospels never knew Jesus and never witnessed any of the events they describe. What's more, there are numerous scenes in the Gospels that make you just scratch your head and say, gee, what could possibly be the source of this information. How could the Gospel writers, or for that matter anyone, know that? Here are some of the most glaring examples:

Joseph's Dreams: Joseph has a dream in which an angel tells him not to get upset over the fact that Mary is pregnant. He tells Joseph that the impregnator is the Holy Spirit and not some other guy. How in the world did Matthew find out about this dream? I doubt that it was the angel who spread the word, and Joseph disappears without explanation after the visit to the temple in Jerusalem when Jesus was twelve years old. Maybe he told Mary, who told someone, who told someone else, etc. (Matthew 1: 20-21) An angel also appears to Joseph in a dream to tell him to flee with Jesus and Mary to Egypt so that King Herod doesn't find Jesus and kill him. (Matthew 2 13-15) When Herod dies, Joseph has another dream in which an angel appears to tell him that it is now safe to return "to the land of Israel." When he gets there, he's afraid that it's still too dangerous to stay there, and he's warned in yet another dream to go to "the district of Galilee." (Matthew 2 19-23) Who could have possibly been the source of information about these dreams and angelic apparitions?

Other Angel Scenes: The Angel Gabriel appears to Zechariah to tell him that his wife, Elizabeth, will conceive and give birth to John the Baptist. Nobody else is there during the colloquy. (Luke 1:11-23)

The Angel Gabriel also appears to Mary to tell her that the Holy Spirit will impregnate her and that she will conceive and give birth to "the Son of God." Once again, they are the only ones present. (Luke: 1: 26-38)

The Nativity Scene: An angel appears to a group of shepherds, announcing that "a Savior" is born "who is Christ the Lord. And this will be a sign for you: you will find a baby wrapped in swaddling cloths and lying in a manger." Then "a multitude" of angels appears to the shepherds, praising God. The only ones there are the angels and the shepherds. Who was the source of information for this scene? It would have to be the shepherds, right? At the manger the only people present were Mary, Joseph, Jesus and the shepherds. Once again, who was the source of information for this scene? It wasn't Jesus. He was a newborn infant. It also wasn't Joseph, so it would have to be Mary or the shepherds. Luke says the shepherds "made known the saying that had been told them concerning this child," while "Mary treasured up all these things, pondering them in her heart." (Luke 2: 8-19) OK.

Suppose the shepherds did tell a lot of people about all that they heard and saw. This information would have to have been transferred to a long line of people before it finally got to Luke, who then writes about it maybe eighty years later.

The Wise Men Visit the Baby Jesus: Here we have a very similar issue to the one described above. How do we know that the Wise Men visited the Baby Jesus and gave him gold, frankincense and myrrh? We are also told that the Wise Men had a secret meeting with King Herod. Who was the source for what happened at this secret meeting—Herod or the Wise Men? The Wise Men also have a dream, warning them not to return to Herod and tell him where the Baby Jesus is. How do we know about that dream? (Matthew 2: 1-12)

Note: All of the scenes described above concerning events around the time of Jesus' birth, take place 50 to 80 years before the Gospels of Matthew and Luke are written and lack any credible sources. Here are a few more examples of scenes with no credible sources:

The Devil Tempts Jesus in the Desert: This scene is in Matthew (4: 1-11), Mark (1:12-13) and Luke (4: 1-13). John apparently didn't get the memo. We're in the desert, and nobody else is there except Jesus and the Devil. Who's the source? I'm hearing crickets on this one.

The Death of John the Baptist: How do we know that Salome's mother told her to ask King Herod to give her the head of John the Baptist on a platter? Who got the word out on this? The mother? The girl? Herod? Did some of Herod's guests know and spread the word? How do we know that Herod was sorry he beheaded John? (Matthew 14: 6-12) Mark says that he "was exceedingly sorry." (Mark 6: 21-28)

Jesus in Gethsemane: How do we know what Jesus said in his prayer to the Father? The apostles with him were asleep. (Matthew 26: 36-46) (Mark 14: 35-42), (Luke 22: 39-46)

Judas Regrets His Betrayal of Jesus: How in the world do we know about the conversation between Judas and the chief priests and elders when Judas had second thoughts about his betrayal of Jesus and wanted to return the thirty pieces of silver? Did Judas brief one of the disciples on the meeting before going out and hanging himself? (Matthew 27: 3-5)

Jesus Before Pilate: Similarly how do we know what Jesus and Pontius Pilate said to one another? In the scene as reported by Matthew, Mark and Luke, who was listening to that conversation besides the chief priests and the elders? Did they report the scene somehow? Were they the reliable sources? (Matthew 27: 11-14) (Mark 15: 1-5), (Luke 23: 1-3) In the scene as reported by John (18: 33-38), the conversation is much more extensive, and Jesus and Pilate appear to be alone since we are told that the Jews who had arrested Jesus and had taken him to Pilate "did not enter the governor's headquarters, so that they would not be defiled, but could eat the Passover." (18: 28).

The fact is that we have absolutely no information on Jesus that would satisfy a journalistic standard of reporting. We have no eyewitness reports, let alone corroborated eyewitness reports, and we have no reliable documentary evidence about Jesus' life. As a result, there is simply no reason to believe anything that is described in the Gospels. If you are an educated and intelligent person who decides what is factual and true based on a journalistic standard of evidence, then you have to abandon that standard if you are to believe anything in the Gospels. In other words, you accept the truth of the Gospels as a matter of faith. You believe that the Gospels are divinely inspired. So when it comes to a scene or an event that nobody could possibly know about, that's no problem at all. The Holy Spirit told the Gospel writers all about it. Who witnessed the conversation between Jesus and Satan in the desert? Why the Holy Spirit did, of course.

This is not to say that there did not exist a charismatic preacher who inspired followers and set in motion the Christian faith. It is to say, however, that we do not really know anything definitive about him. We do not know what Jesus thought, said or did except through the rather distant and dubious lens of the Gospels, i.e., unreliable accounts written by proselytizers and advocates of Jesus decades after he is said to have died. Imagine if we just heard about Watergate for the first time a couple of weeks ago, and imagine if the source of the Watergate story were G. Gordon Liddy. I think we'd get a pretty different account of that episode than the one we have from Woodward and Bernstein.

Now here's the funny thing: you can accept on faith everything in the Gospels. You can believe that Jesus was the Son of God, that he died for our sins and that he rose from the dead. You can also believe in and try to emulate everything that he taught. There is still no reasonable basis for maintaining that Jesus started a church in the sense of formally creating a religious institution, and he obviously had nothing to do with how the Catholic Church developed after his death over a couple of hundred years from loosely affiliated groups of Christian believers into a centralized, state-sponsored institutional religion.

HERESY

One of the best ways to tell that a grassroots religious movement is turning into a full-blown religious institution with divinely inspired dogma is the demand for orthodoxy. It's just not possible to establish the one true religion and tolerate different beliefs. Those two things don't go together. No way. No how.

No doubt (that's a nice phrase), the insistence on orthodoxy is there from the beginning in most religious movements, especially among the movement's leaders. But the requirement to adhere to a codified set of precepts and beliefs increases as a religion becomes more established. Interestingly, if you aren't familiar with what a particular religion's beliefs are, it's hard to know what's orthodox and what's heretical in any given dispute. Sometimes the disputes are just plain silly.

One of the first disputes in the early Christian church was over when to celebrate the resurrection of Jesus. The Christians in the East celebrated it around Passover. The Roman Christians thought it was a good idea to celebrate it every Sunday, believing I suppose that you can't have too much of a good thing. Obviously the Romans lost that battle, much to the future dismay of Easter egg manufacturers and chicken farmers. In 325 the First Council of Nicaea decided that Easter should be celebrated on the first Sunday after the full moon following the northern hemisphere's vernal equinox. But of course. I don't know why that wasn't obvious to everybody from the beginning.

While the desire to celebrate Jesus' resurrection every Sunday rather than once a year hardly rises to the level of heresy, the disagreement over the correct observance of Easter was apparently rather contentious. Indeed, when it comes to debates over what is orthodox Christian or Catholic belief and what is heretical, the outcome throughout history has been more than just contentious. It's often been a matter of life and death. Of course, all such discussions are forever cast in the light of the historic irony that Christianity was originally viewed by Jewish orthodox believers as a Jewish heresy. This is certainly the point of view of the Pharisees and the Sadducees who opposed Jesus and his teachings. Although their opposition is given an exceedingly negative spin by the Gospel writers, they were simply doing to Jesus exactly what Christian proponents of orthodoxy would later do to individuals with divergent views of the Christian faith. Think, for example, of the Pharisees' reaction to Jesus healing on the Sabbath, let alone his claim that he was the Messiah, which they viewed as blasphemy. In fact, that was the crime for which they arrested him and wanted him to be executed. Ironically, that very same fate would befall Christian heretics throughout the centuries.

The person responsible for kicking early Christian orthodoxy into high gear is St. Irenaeus of Lyons. He wrote a five-volume work called *Against Heresies*, attacking Gnosticism, a rather exotic set of beliefs that in its varying forms often disagreed with itself and certainly diverged dramatically from the true Christian faith. Gnosticism is all but extinct now, but it was a big deal then, and its believers thought that they knew the real story on such important topics as how the world was created, the origin of evil and how you got to heaven.

In his treatise Irenaeus also asserted the doctrine of papal authority and apostolic succession and proclaimed that Rome was the place where the church was "founded and organized" by the apostles Peter and Paul. It's pretty clear, that wasn't true. Christian communities were already established in Rome before either Peter or Paul would have arrived. In fact, there isn't even proof that Peter went to Rome, although, based on rather dubious circumstantial evidence, church and papal historians believe that he did and claim that he was crucified upside down by the Emperor Nero. These same people also believe that Paul was martyred there as well, although the only evidence for that is what is politely called "early Christian tradition."

In addition to his pronouncements on papal authority and the centrality of Rome, Irenaeus also declared that there had to be four canonical Gospels—it was impossible for there to be any other number. There couldn't be three or five, for example. There had to be four, and those four were Matthew, Mark, Luke and John. How's that for absolute certitude! As ridiculous as this idea is, it perfectly captures the orthodox mindset. Orthodoxy says there is only one truth, and I know what it is. It doesn't matter how absurd or crazy that truth may seem to other people or if other people have different beliefs. Different beliefs are a threat and must be eradicated. The people who espouse those beliefs have no right to profess them and should be ostracized. Their leaders should be killed.

Just as Jesus was a heretic to the Pharisees, the Christians were heretics to the Romans. But when the Roman emperor Constantine legalized Christianity in 313 and became its champion, he ensured the continuity of the Christian religion and virtually guaranteed that Christians would have their opportunity to persecute others as they themselves had been persecuted.

In 325, Constantine convened the First Council of Nicaea. In addition to deciding when Easter should be celebrated, as mentioned above, the council, which was composed of a few hundred bishops, issued a document, the Nicene Creed, which codified orthodox

Christian beliefs. The few bishops who disagreed with parts of the creed and refused to support it were excommunicated and exiled. This group included Arius, who believed that Jesus was created by God the Father and was inferior to him rather than being eternal and equal. Following the council, Constantine ordered that Arius's writings be burned and that anyone who was later found with them should be executed.

The next major step in establishing the power and preeminence of Christianity was the edict of Thessalonica in 380, issued by the Roman Emperor Theodosius. The edict required all Christians to embrace orthodoxy and established a legal basis for persecuting heresy. Orthodoxy is defined as subjection to papal authority and adherence to the Nicene Creed. The edict authorized all orthodox believers to go by "the title of Catholic Christians" and proclaimed that all who did not adhere to orthodox beliefs were to "be branded with the ignominious name of heretics. . . . They will suffer in the first place the chastisement of the divine condemnation and in the second the punishment of our authority which in the accordance of the will of heaven we will decide to inflict."

One would imagine that "divine condemnation" means eternal punishment in hell. As far as "the second punishment" is concerned, that could mean excommunication, exile, imprisonment, torture or death. The first person executed for heresy was Priscillian, the bishop of Avila. He was at odds with a number of other bishops over his beliefs and practices. Priscillian's heretical practices included allowing women to worship with men, fasting on Sunday and taking the Eucharist home. For these and other heretical crimes he and six of his followers were beheaded in 385.

According to Tradition...
Legend Has It

When you read the history of the Catholic Church, a certain phrase pops up with some frequency: "according to tradition." Similarly, you will read the words, "is believed" or "is said." These are all weasel words, meaning that we have no historical proof of what follows, but the church has said it is true, and since we have no evidence contradicting what the church says, we continue to believe that it is true as well. Here are some striking examples:

"According to tradition," Jesus was born on December 25. The *Baltimore Catechism*, frets about the wintry weather and empathizes that "the little Infant Jesus must have suffered greatly from the cold." For the record, the average temperature in December in Bethlehem is about 50 degrees Fahrenheit.

"According to tradition," the Apostle Peter was crucified upside down in Rome. There is absolutely no proof that this happened. All we know is that many years later church leaders believed that he was and said that he was. We do not even know for sure that Peter died in Rome or how much time he spent there. Amazingly many historians accept the tradition as fact.

"According to tradition," the Apostle Paul was beheaded in Rome. Same story as above. No proof. Just people saying so many years later.

"According to tradition," Peter functioned as pope as did his successors, i.e., Linus, Anacietus, Clement, Evaristus, Alexander, Sixtus,

and so on. Actually there was no person with true centralized authority over Christians until Constantine gave his stamp of approval to
Christianity. What's more, he and his immediate successors as Roman
emperor were much more important than whoever was pope at the
time.

"According to tradition," the first thirty-one popes were martyred.
Now that's a dangerous job! Just imagine if the first thirty-one presi-
dents of the United States had been assassinated. That would be every
president from George Washington to Herbert Hoover. Wow! That's
unbelievable! Precisely. It turns out it's not true. Not even close. There
were long periods during which Christians were not persecuted. In
fact, among the early popes there are only a few who we actually know
were killed. We know that Pontian, the 18th pope (230-35), was exiled
to the island of Sardinia by the Roman emperor Maximinus Thrax,
where he died of exposure and starvation, We also know that Sixtus
II, the 24th pope (257-58), was killed by Roman soldiers for refusing to
sacrifice to the Roman gods. Martin, the 74th pope, (649-55) was also
martyred. He was exiled by the Roman emperor Constans II and died,
like Pontian, of exposure and starvation.

As you can see from the foregoing examples, "according to tradition" refers to stuff that could have actually happened. In some cases,
we just don't know if it did or not while in other cases it's pretty clear
that it did not happen. When it comes to "legend," we're in a whole
different ballgame. Legend often refers to stuff that couldn't possibly
happen—like miracles and other supernatural occurrences—or to the
lives of people, often saints, who never even existed.

"Legend has it" that while the Apostle Peter was fleeing Rome to
escape the persecution of Nero he encountered Jesus carrying a cross
on the Via Appia. When he asked Jesus where he was going, Jesus replied, "To Rome, to be crucified again." Supposedly this turned Peter

around, and he went back to Rome to die for the Christian faith.

"Legend has it" that St. Christopher devoted himself to helping people cross a dangerous river. That's why he's venerated as the patron saint of travelers. One day a little boy came over to him and asked him to carry him across the river. For some reason nobody has ever bothered to ask why a little boy would be traveling by himself or why he would want to cross a dangerous river. Anyway, as Christopher is carrying him across, the river becomes increasingly rough and the boy gets heavier and heavier so that Christopher can barely make it across. When he reaches the other side, Christopher says to the boy, "I do not think the whole world could have been as heavy on my shoulders as you were."

Then the boy says, "You had on your shoulders not only the whole world but Him who made it. I am Christ your king, whom you are serving by this work." Then the boy disappears.

"Legend has it" that St. Sebastian, a Christian officer in the Roman army, was so good that whenever he spoke he was immediately bathed in light. In fact, he was so very, very good that God granted him the very special privilege of being martyred twice. The first time the Emperor Diocletian ordered his execution, and he was famously tied semi-naked to a post and shot with arrows. Now, what most people don't know is that Sebastian didn't die from all of those arrow wounds but instead was miraculously rescued. He then marched right back to the emperor and told him to knock off all of this persecution nonsense. Instead of knocking it off, Diocletian had Sebastian beaten to death. This time the martyrdom took, and Sebastian won his heavenly reward.

"Legend has it" that while St. Ursula was on a pilgrimage to Rome along with 11,000 virgins (yes, 11,000!), she and all 11,000 of her virgin companions were massacred in Cologne by Huns. In 1969 St.

Ursula had her feast day removed from the church calendar because the church decided that she never existed—I assume that applies to the 11,000 virgins as well.

Quick hits: "Legend has it" that . . .

- St. Patrick drove the snakes out of Ireland.

- St. George slayed a dragon.

- St. Nicholas delivered presents every December to all the little boys and girls who had been good throughout the year.

- When he was imprisoned for his faith, St. Valentine gave religious instructions to his jailor's blind daughter. Just before he was martyred, he sent the little girl a note in which he told her to always stay close to God. He signed the note, "From your Valentine." When the little girl opened the note, she found a yellow crocus inside, and instantly her sight was restored. What a lucky little girl! Not only could she see for the first time in her entire life, but she had the great, historic distinction of receiving the very first Valentine card.

HERSTORY

WHERE ARE THE WOMEN?

When you read the history of the Catholic Church, if you didn't know any better, you might think that there were almost no women walking the face of the earth except for a few virgin/martyrs. The absence of women is positively creepy throughout church history. Of course, it's not surprising at all. Not a single woman has ever held a position of power in the Catholic Church or in most of the other Christian denominations. That's zero women in more than 2,000 years. Of course, if you can't be ordained a priest or a minister, it's impossible to have any institutional power.

When you think of it, women have a lot going against them as far as the Christian religion is concerned. God the Father isn't human, but he refers to himself as male. Jesus is a man too. Imagine what a difference it would have made if God had sent his only begotten daughter to die on a cross for our sins. Also, I can't prove it, but I'll bet that when the Holy Spirit appears as a dove, he's a cock instead of a hen.

Eve was made from Adam's rib and is blamed for the fall of man. That's why women are subject to men and suffer the excruciating pain of childbirth. In the Old Testament women are basically chattel. According to the law of the Old Testament God, fathers can sell their daughters into slavery. In the New Testament, Paul states that wives must be subordinate to their husbands and that "it is shameful for a woman to speak in church." In his treatise *On the Apparel of Women*, Tertullian, one of the so-called "church fathers," makes the extraordinarily crazy statement that women's "ornamentation," i.e., jewelry, perfume and makeup, was given to them by the fallen angels—that would be Satan and his pals—and that through the introduction of these seductive arts, women share in the "ignominy" of the angels' fall. He also says that women should dress in as plain and drab a manner as possible and go about "mourning and repentant" to help "expiate" the sin of Eve, which they bear. The insidious implication of these statements on women's attire is that if a man feels sexual attraction towards a woman and acts on it—maybe even against the woman's will—it is the woman's fault, not his, because the woman would have seduced him. So rape is the fault of women, not men. Actually Tertullian is quite explicit in that regard, calling women "the devil's gateway." Burkas, anyone?

There is a seemingly endless series of statements throughout history by popes, saints, doctors of the church and assorted clergymen vilifying and demonizing women. Here are some samples, including "the devil's gateway" remark from Tertullian:

St. Irenaeus

"Nature and the law place the woman in a subordinate condition to the man."
—*Fragment*, No. 32.

Tertullian

"Do you not know that you are (each) an Eve? The sentence of God on this sex of yours lives in this age: the guilt must of necessity live too. *You* are the devil's gateway: *you* are the unsealer of that (forbidden) tree: *you* are the first deserter of the divine law: *you* are she who persuaded him whom the devil was not valiant enough to attack. *You* destroyed so easily God's image, man. On account of *your* desert—that is, death—even the Son of God had to die."

—*On the Apparel of Women*, Chapter 1. Introduction. Modesty in Apparel Becoming to Women, in Memory of the Introduction of Sin into the World Through a Woman.

St. Clement of Alexandria

"By no manner of means are women to be allotted to uncover and exhibit any part of their person, lest both fall, the men by being excited to look, they by drawing on themselves the eyes of the men."

—*The Paedagogus (The Instructor)*, Book 2, Chapter 2, On Drinking

St. John Chrysostom

"As all men died through one, because that one sinned, so the whole female race transgressed, because the woman was in the transgression. Let her not however grieve. God has given her no small consolation, that of childbearing."

—*Homily 9 on First Timothy*

St. Jerome

"If [according to the Apostle Paul] it is good not to touch a woman, it is bad to touch one: for there is no opposite to goodness but badness."

—*Against Jovinianus,* Book 1.

St. Ambrose

"The virtue of silence, especially in Church, is very great. Let no sentence of the divine lessons escape you; if you give ear, restrain your voice, utter no word with your lips which you would wish to recall, but let your boldness to speak be sparing. For in truth in much speaking there is abundance of sin." (Proverbs 10:19) To the murderer it was said: 'You have sinned, be silent' (Genesis 4:7) that he might not sin more; but to the virgin it must be said, 'Be silent lest you sin.'"

—*Concerning Virginity.* Book III, Chapter 3.

St. Augustine

"The woman together with her own husband is the image of God, so that that whole substance may be one image; but when she is referred separately to her quality of *help-meet,* which regards the woman herself alone, then she is not the image of God."

—*On the Trinity,* Book XII, Chapter 7.

St. Thomas Aquinas

"As regards the individual nature, woman is defective and misbegotten, for the active force in the male seed tends to the production of a perfect likeness in the masculine sex; while the production of woman comes from defect in the active force or from some material indisposition, or even from some external influence, such as that of a south wind, which is moist, as the Philosopher [i.e., Aristotle] observes."

—*Summa Theologica* I, Q. 92, Art. 1

"Just as it is unbecoming for a woman to wear man's clothes, so it is unbecoming for her to adorn herself inordinately. Now the former is a sin, for it is written: 'A woman shall not be clothed with man's apparel, neither shall a man use woman's apparel.' (Deuteronomy 22:5) Therefore it seems also that the excessive adornment of women is a mortal sin."

—*Summa Theologica*, II-II, Q.169, Art. 2.

The idea that women are inferior to men was incorporated into a set of laws in the 12th century by Johannes Gratian. His *Decretum Gratiani* became part of official church law, i.e., Canon Law, in the 13th century and continued to be in effect until 1918 when Pope Benedict XV established a new Code of Canon Law. Despite the new code, there was no change whatsoever in the status of women within the church.

In 1983 the code was revised again and included some expansion in the functions that women could perform within the church, including serving as lectors or cantors at Mass. Of course, women were still excluded from the priesthood and still have no position of authority within the church.

The Catholic Encyclopedia includes an essay titled "Woman," which refers repeatedly with consummate male awkwardness to the "woman question." In the essay the following statements appear:

"The female sex is in some respects inferior to the male sex, both as regards body and soul."

"The most manly man and the most feminine woman are the most perfect types of their sexes."

"Man is called by the Creator to [the] position of leader, as is shown by his entire bodily and intellectual make-up."

Quoting Pope Leo XIII—

"The husband is the ruler of the family and the head of the wife; the woman as flesh of his flesh and bone of his bone is to be subordinate and obedient to the husband."

"Ulpian [the Roman jurist] gives a celebrated rule of law which most canonists have embodied in their works: 'Women are ineligible to all civil and public offices, and therefore they cannot be judges, nor hold a magistracy, nor act as lawyers, judicial intercessors, or procurators. . . . The reason given by canonists for this prohibition is not the levity, weakness, or fragility of the female sex, but the preservation of the modesty and dignity peculiar to woman."

"The social duties of the woman may . . . be designated as motherhood. . . . The completely developed feminine personality is thus to be found in the mother."

It's instructive to note that the online edition of the Encyclopedia www.newadvent.com is simply a transcription of the 1912 edition. The only update to its essay on "Woman"—Breaking News, everyone— is that the editor recommends "a prayerful reading" of Blessed Pope John Paul II's 1988 apostolic letter *Mulieris Dignatatem*, "The Dignity of Women." In the letter the pope uses the story of Adam and Eve to teach us about the true role of women. He calls the story a symbolic narrative, but his application of the story is more insidious than if he were to act as if this fairy tale actually happened. He basically says that the story of Adam and Eve is a divinely inspired symbolic communication of how sin entered the world, and the particular way that that happened resulted in the "domination" of man over woman.

So the result of sin coming into the world is that men rule over women forever and ever after. How's that? Well, remember the whole thing is mostly Eve's fault because she gave Adam the fruit to eat. So Adam was basically seduced. After all he's a guy, and if a naked woman gives you a piece of fruit to eat, what else can you do but eat it? John Paul II is careful to quote the Apostle Paul to further drive home this point. In his epistle to Timothy, Paul says, "Adam was formed first, then Eve; and Adam was not deceived, but the woman was deceived and became a transgressor." The pope then proceeds to base his extremely learned dissertation on the true role of women on this utterly preposterous premise.

Ironically, the letter is most instructive on this point. This is how religion works. Its MO is to assert an absolutely absurd and ridiculous premise and claim that the truth of that premise has been divinely revealed. Then it bases an infallible teaching on this divinely inspired premise that everybody has to believe and practice. In this case the teaching is that men are meant by God to dominate women. It doesn't matter that this would mean that God is a woman hater, a misogynist, and that he is advocating bigotry and discrimination against women. No, say the men who run the church. This is the very nature of reality revealed to us by God. Who are you to question it?

When the Catholic Church states that its teachings are unalterable, it really means it. The rather comical anachronism of the 1912 Encyclopedia pales in comparison to John Paul's absurd reassertion of the Garden of Eden story as the basis for women's subservience to men.

What can I say? The relentless misogyny of the church for ages and ages—I don't mean this as a criticism, but it makes me wonder why there are any female Catholics. It also makes me embarrassed to be a human being and ashamed to have been born a man.

Postscript to "Where Are the Women?" In July 2010 the Vatican belatedly issued a statement announcing that it was revising its internal procedures for policing pedophile priests, calling child sexual abuse a "grave crime." However, in the statement it chose to cite the ordination of women as a "grave crime" as well, establishing a moral equivalence between the ordination of women and the sexual abuse of children.

In his Holy Thursday homily on April 5, 2012, Pope Benedict XVI condemned the "disobedience" of priests who call for the ordination of women, stating that these priests are "disregarding definitive decisions of the Church's Magisterium" and citing the fact that "Blessed Pope John Paul II stated irrevocably that the church has received no authority from the Lord" to ordain women.

The beat goes on.

There's Something about Mary

There is one woman that the Catholic Church absolutely loves—you might even say adores. That's Mary, the Mother of God, i.e., the Mother of Jesus. So there's this huge inverse relationship between Mary and just about every other woman who ever lived. Mary is venerated, while women throughout history have been denigrated by the Catholic Church. But here's the thing: Is Mary really a woman? It's kind of hard to think of her that way. She's really more like a goddess.

First of all, we really don't know anything about her. As I've pointed out, the Gospels were written anywhere from sixty to more than a hundred years after Jesus was born, and there are only a few references in them to Mary anyway. What's more, there are a number of scenes where, as I've noted, there is no credible source. Almost all of the scenes involving Mary before Jesus was born or when he was a child come from Luke's Gospel:

- The angel Gabriel appears to Mary to tell her that she will be impregnated by the Holy Spirit and give birth to the Messiah.

- Mary visits Elizabeth, who will be the mother of John the Baptist, and recites a formally constructed hymn of praise, the Magnificat.

- She gives birth to Jesus. Shepherds and angels show up.

- Mary and Joseph take the baby Jesus to the temple in Jerusalem for a purification ceremony.

- Mary and Joseph take Jesus to the temple in Jerusalem when Jesus is twelve, somehow leave without him and have to go back to get him. When they find Jesus and Mary tells him how worried they were, Jesus cops an attitude and says that she should have known that he had to be out on his own preaching and teaching.

None of these scenes appears in the other Gospels. The Angel Gabriel's visit to Joseph in a dream to inform him of Mary's impregnation by the Holy Spirit, the visit of the Wise Men, the flight to Egypt and the return to Nazareth are from Matthew's Gospel. In John's Gospel we have the story of the wedding feast of Cana, and Mary tells Jesus to fix the wine problem. Matthew, Mark and Luke all tell of an incident where Mary and Jesus' brothers come to where he is preaching and wish to see him, but Jesus is not interested. He says that his disciples are his mother and brothers. (Note: There is a debate over what the relationship of these so-called "brothers" was to Jesus. There is of course no debate about it in the Catholic Church. They maintain Mary's perpetual virginity and say that the "brothers" were Jesus' cousins.)

The only other appearance of Mary in the Gospels is at Jesus' crucifixion. That's according to John. The other three Gospels don't say that she was there. That's it. She's mentioned once in Acts. She's in the room with the disciples when they replace Judas with Mathias. She is never mentioned again. Like Joseph, she just disappears.

When you think about it, it makes sense that Joseph and Mary both have limited roles in the Gospels. Joseph isn't Jesus' father—that's

God, the Father and/or the Holy Spirit since he's the one who impregnated Mary. Joseph is just there at the beginning as a kind of foster father or protector. After that, he isn't needed. So he just drops out of the story. Frankly, after miraculously conceiving and then giving birth to Jesus, Mary isn't needed either. Jesus had to have a mother because, well, everybody has one. In his case, apparently she had to be a virgin. The Catholic Church goes even further and says that she had to be born free of original sin too—that's the Immaculate Conception—and she had to be absolutely perfect and free of sin for her entire life as well. So Mary fills this goddess-like maternal role, but beyond that she's extraneous to the story and to Jesus' mission. He certainly sees it that way since he rebuffs her at the temple when he's twelve and when she approaches him while he's preaching to his disciples.

Fortunately the Catholic Church does step in to give Mary a sendoff befitting the goddess that she is. On the basis of absolutely nothing, the church decided that Mary was assumed into heaven. Assumed. That's what they call it. Does anybody know what that means? How can you be assumed into anything? Does that mean that when she died, her body just disappeared? It just evaporated and went to heaven? Or did Mary never even die in the first place? Was it just sort of time for her to go—and she went? Did she float off into the sky like Jesus did when he ascended into heaven? Or did she have a kind of limo service at her disposal, like Elijah did when he was picked up by the fiery horses with their fiery chariot? I guess we'll just never know.

I also think it's extremely odd that the church waited until 1950 to decide that Mary was assumed into heaven—at least they waited that long to declare infallibly that it is an article of faith. They also waited until 1854 to declare her Immaculate Conception an article of faith. If they were both true, what's up with the incredible delay?

In any event, you do have to give Mary credit. She must have been really annoyed that she only had a cameo role in the Gospels. But, boy, has she been making up for it ever since. Over the centuries she's made more miraculous appearances in more places around the world to more children and mentally ill, delusional people than anybody else. It's not even close. Nobody has come back to us from the other side—in Mary's case you can't say back from the dead—more than she has. I'll bet she's appeared tens of thousands of times. So-called Marian experts have estimated that there have been more than 20,000 Marian apparitions in the last 1,000 years. I'm sure though that nobody knows the actual number. Just think of all the times Mary appeared and people decided to keep it to themselves. I know I would.

There's another nice thing about Mary's appearances. Every time she appears somewhere and the appearance becomes famous, Mary gets a new name. How's that for recognition!

Here are some of Mary's most famous appearances:

Our Lady of Fatima: Hey! That's the name of the elementary school that I went to when I was a kid. Anyway, here's the incredible story: On May 13, 1917, in Fatima, Portugal, Mary appeared to three children—ages seven, nine and ten—while they were tending sheep. This was the first of six monthly appearances—all on the 13th day of the month. According to the oldest child, Lúcia Santos, Mary told the children that they should do penance and make sacrifices. As a result the children engaged in acts of self-mortification, such as flagellation, binding and refusing to drink water. These "sacrifices" are supposedly pleasing to God. They persuade him to forgive dead sinners, reduce their sentence in Purgatory and let them into heaven sooner. Mary also gave the children three secrets, which were to be revealed to the world at a later date.

The monthly apparitions drew huge crowds. There was apparently an expectation that Mary would produce a miracle at some point as proof of her appearances. In October, Lúcia told people in the crowd to look at the sun. Lots of people stared into the sun. They reported that the sun then behaved unusually. It changed color, spun like a wheel and danced around in the sky. While the sun was dancing, the children reported seeing, not only Mary, but Jesus and Joseph too. This was the last of Mary's appearances at Fatima. Also, I don't know if it was embarrassed by its performance or what the story is, but there is no evidence that the sun ever danced again.

The church investigated the apparitions and declared them "worthy of belief." That is the rather curious phrase they use when they decide that it's OK for people to believe that miraculous events have occurred. The two younger children, Jacinta and Francisco, died in the Spanish flu epidemic at the ages of nine and ten, respectively, and were beatified by Pope John Paul II in 2000.

Lúcia became a nun and continued to have apparitions of Mary throughout her life. On at least one occasion she also had an apparition of Jesus. He taught her two prayers and gave her another secret message. So far as I know, the content of Jesus' message has never been made public. Lúcia revealed the first two secret messages of Fatima in 1941. Message number one was a vision of hell. Message number two basically said that people should devote themselves to the Immaculate Heart of Mary to help out dead souls and that the world should repent or God would send a war to punish everybody. Apparently that was World War II. Mary was particularly interested in making sure that the people of Russia consecrated themselves to her Immaculate Heart. If they didn't, she said that lots of people would be killed and entire nations would be annihilated—sounds like a prediction of nuclear war. Thank God that hasn't happened yet.

In 2000 Pope John Paul II revealed the third secret of Fatima. It was essentially an apocalyptic vision in which an angel repeatedly shouts the word, "Penance" and the Pope, bishops and priests are martyred. Conspiracy theories have grown up claiming that this was not the real secret message or maybe only part of the secret message and that the church is refusing to make public the transcription of an apocalyptic message from Mary.

Lucia died in 2005 at the age of 97. In 2008 Pope Benedict XVI waived the five-year waiting period and began Lucia's beatification process.

Our Lady of Lourdes: In 1858 in Lourdes, France, Mary appeared repeatedly to Bernadette Soubirous, a fourteen-year-old girl. The appearances took place by a cave. When word spread about the apparitions, water was drawn from a nearby spring and distributed to sick and disabled people. There were many reported cures. People travel to Lourdes to this very day to be cured of their ills by drinking or bathing in the water. The church has validated the apparitions and confirmed many of the cures. Bernadette died in 1879 at the age of 35. She was canonized in 1933 by Pope Pius XI. You can buy a small bottle of Lourdes water for just $24.99 at www.directfromlourdes.com/. The bottle is inscribed with a beautiful 3D plaque that shows Bernadette kneeling before Mary. The site maintains that you are purchasing authentic Lourdes water and that it is fresh and safe to drink.

Our Lady of Mount Carmel: According to tradition, or maybe I should say, legend has it, that around the middle of the 13th century Mary appeared in Cambridge, England, to Simon Stock, a Carmelite monk. She told him that if you are wearing a brown scapular when you die, you are sure of going to heaven. Later a belief developed that if you died wearing the brown scapular, Mary would personally make sure that you got out of Purgatory really fast—actually the Saturday after you died. So, if at all possible, it obviously would work out best if you died really late on a Friday evening. I didn't even know that they had days of the week in the afterlife. Actually even the church doubts that this apparition ever occurred, but it still highly recommends wearing a brown scapular, and Simon Stock is still a saint. A scapular originally referred to a sleeveless cloth garment that monks wore over their heads, and it really wasn't all that fashionable. It looked a little, well, monkish. But that's changed, and now it's just a small cloth necklace, so you can wear a scapular all of the time without anybody even knowing about it, no problem. That way you make sure you keep your ticket to heaven with you at all times.

Our Lady of Guadalupe: In 1531 Mary appeared to Juan Diego in the desert near Mexico City. She wanted to let him know that she'd like a church built there. Despite doubts that Juan Diego existed, he was canonized in 2002.

Our Lady of Laus: From 1664 to 1718, in Saint-Étienne-le-Laus, France, Mary repeatedly appeared to Benoîte Rencurel, a shepherd. The Vatican approved the apparitions in 2008. In 2009 Benoîte was declared "Venerable."

Our Lady of the Miraculous Medal: In 1830, Mary appeared to Catherine Labouré in a convent in Paris. Catherine had previously seen apparitions of St. Vincent and Jesus. In the first encounter with Mary, Catherine heard her speak to her. In her second encounter Mary gave Catherine the design for a medal. Catherine was canonized in 1947.

Our Lady of Good Help: In 1859 Mary appeared in Bay Settlement, Wisconsin, to Adele Brise, a Belgian immigrant. Her message was to pray for the conversion of sinners. In 2010 the bishop of Green Bay approved the apparition, but it has not yet received formal Vatican approval.

Our Lady of Hope: In 1871 Mary appeared to a group of children in Pontmain, France. They saw her floating in the sky. At one point a banner appeared at her feet with a message about the importance of prayer. The town was about to be invaded by the Prussian army, but immediately after the apparition, the army inexplicably turned back. The church has officially approved this apparition.

Our Lady of Akita: In 1973 in a remote area outside of Akita, Japan, Mary appeared to Sister Agnes Katsuko Sasagawa. Mary's message was to pray the rosary or bad things will happen. In addition to the apparition a statue of Mary started to cry. The crying was televised nationally. Over a six-year period the statue cried 101 times. I really wish somebody would find a way to cheer up that statue. The statue also got the stigmata, i.e., its hands had wounds like the crucified Christ. Sister Agnes supposedly got the stigmata too. In 1988 Cardinal Joseph Ratzinger declared the apparition and the weeping statue "worthy of belief."

Our Lady of Cuapa: In 1980, Mary appeared repeatedly in Cuapa, Nicaragua, during the civil war between the Contras and the Sandinista government, to Bernardo Martinez, a man who worked at the local church. Before the first apparition Bernardo saw the statue of Mary in the church light up by itself. When Mary appeared, she told Bernardo to pray the rosary, promote peace and burn bad books. I wonder what

Mary thinks of the First Amendment? Anyway, based on this information the auxiliary Bishop of Managua, who was pro-Contra, burned books associated with the Sandinista government.

All of these apparitions create new devotions to Mary. There are also numerous devotions not generated by her appearances. These include devotions to:

Our Lady of Sorrows:

According to www.churchsupplywarehouse.com this devotional title along with "the Sorrowful Mother or Mother of Sorrows (Latin: *Mater Dolorosa*), Our Lady of the Seven Sorrows or Our Lady of the Seven Dolours are names by which the Blessed Virgin Mary is referred to in relation to sorrows in her life. Under this title, she is the patron saint of Slovakia, the state of Mississippi, the Congregation of Holy Cross [and] Mola di Bari, Italy." Mary's Seven Sorrows are:

1. The prophecy of Simeon

2. The flight into Egypt

3. The loss of the Child Jesus in the temple. (I'm sorry, Mary, but I still can't figure out how you and Joseph went home without Jesus. Shouldn't you know if your child is with you or not?)

4. The meeting of Jesus and Mary on the Way of the Cross (Sorry again, but I can't find this meeting in the Gospels.)

5. The Crucifixion

6. The taking down of the Body of Jesus from the Cross

7. The burial of Jesus

You can buy a picture (artist's rendering, of course) of Our Lady of Sorrows from www.churchsupplywarehouse.com for $125. Check for prices on pictures of the other devotions.

Our Lady of Perpetual Help (aka Our Lady of Perpetual Succor): This devotion is based on a painted wooden icon that depicts Mary holding the Baby Jesus. There are two angels floating around in the picture as well. They're both holding onto instruments used in Jesus' torture and execution. The Archangel Michael is holding a lance and a sponge, while the Archangel Gabriel is holding a cross and nails. The angels have scared the Baby Jesus, and he has run to his mother for help. You can get a high-resolution JPEG of this image from www.restoredtraditions.com for just $15; a higher resolution JPEG is $50. They have JPEGs available for most of the devotions.

The Immaculate Heart of Mary: This is a devotion to Mary that focuses on the spiritual life of Mary, her perfect love for God and her love for her son, Jesus. As the Immaculate Heart, Mary is depicted with her heart exposed, like the Sacred Heart of Jesus. The heart is typically pierced by seven wounds and wrapped in roses. The Immaculate Heart appears on the Miraculous Medal. On the medal the heart is pierced by a sword.

The New Eve: This is a new devotion to Mary as an expectant mother. There is a statue portraying Mary as the New Eve in which Mary is well into her last trimester. Go to the St. Anthony's Guild of Rutherford, NJ website at and take a look at the statue. I don't know. I'm not usually attracted to pregnant women, but I think Mary is looking pretty sexy here. I'm just being honest. www.anthonian.org/resources/marythe-new-eve

Our Lady, Star of the Sea: This is a devotion to Mary as a guide to fishermen and others traveling on the sea. There's an Our Lady Star of the Sea church in Staten Island. Actually, there are quite a few Our Lady Star of the Sea churches around the country. Some of them use the original Latin title, *Stella Maris*. There's one in Philly—my old hometown.

I should add that Our Lady protects other types of travel too. For example, Our Lady of Loreto protects pilots, so that should help out all of us frequent flyers. FYI: "Loreto" refers to the house in which Mary was born. How's that? Well, here's the explanation c/o www.catholicfire.blogspot.com: "The title Our Lady of Loreto refers to the Holy House of Loreto, the house in which Mary was born, and where the Annunciation occurred, and to an ancient statue of Our Lady which is found there. Tradition says that a band of angels scooped up the little house from the Holy Land, and transported it first to Tersato, Dalmatia in 1291, Reananti in 1294, and finally to Loreto, Italy where it has been for centuries. It was this flight that led to her patronage of people involved in aviation." Actually that little explanation clears up everything, including why Our Lady of Loreto is the patron of pilots. It's because angels flew her house to Loreto, Italy. OK.

There are lots of other devotional names of Mary. These include Mary as the Seat of Wisdom (the Throne of Wisdom), the Ark of the New Covenant, the Mediatrix, the Co-Redemptrix, Virgin of Tenderness, Holy Virgin of Virgins, Cause of Our Joy, Queen of Peace, Our Lady of All Nations, Our Lady of Victory; Mary, Help of Christians and Our Lady of the Rosary. I could go on, but I won't.

Of course, the primary devotion to Mary is praying the rosary. According to Pope Leo XII, known as the "Rosary Pope" because he issued eleven encyclicals and five apostolic letters on the rosary: "the Rosary is the most excellent form of prayer and the most efficacious means of attaining eternal life. It is the remedy for all our evils, the root of all our blessings. There is no more excellent way of praying."

There are numerous religious orders of nuns, priests and brothers dedicated to Mary. These include the Sisters, Servants of the Immaculate Heart of Mary; the Marist Fathers and Brothers; the Sisters of Charity of the Blessed Virgin Mary; the Marianists; the Congregation of Marians of the Immaculate Conception; the Maryknoll Sisters; the Franciscan Friars of Mary Immaculate; the Missionary Oblates of Mary Immaculate; the Brothers of Mercy of Our Lady of Perpetual Help; and the Sisters of Notre Dame de Namur.

There are also numerous lay organizations that are dedicated to Mary. These include the Blue Army of Our Lady of Fatima, the Legion of Mary, the Sodality of Our Lady, Our Lady's Rosary Makers, the Secular Order of the Servants of Mary and the Secular Order of Discalced Carmelites. In case, you're wondering, "discalced" means "barefoot." This was St. Teresa of Avila's idea. She thought that going barefoot would signify a return to how the original Carmelites went about their business and that it would represent an additional level of austerity and self-sacrifice. Obviously Teresa was right. Just try running out "discalced" to your mailbox in the middle of a big February snowstorm, and you'll get the point right away.

So what can I say to sum it all up? I would simply say that there is definitely something about Mary. Some people get mad when you say she's adored. They say the Catholic Church doesn't support adoration of Mary. Adoration is only for God. Well, whatever you want to call it, Mary is giving her Son, Jesus, and God, the Father, a pretty good run for their money when it comes to adoration.

And just think: When Mary miraculously conceived Jesus through the power of the Holy Spirit, she was probably no more than twelve years old.

FUN FACTS AND
QUOTABLE QUOTES

Fun Facts about the Catholic Church

Here are some fun facts about the Catholic Church that I've gathered from its rich and illustrious history. Obviously this is a highly selective list. So much has happened over the last 2,000 years that there is really almost an unlimited supply of fun facts. This is just my list. I invite everybody to make their own list. It's a great way to kill time on a rainy Sunday afternoon or maybe while you're waiting for the major league baseball season to start. It's also a tremendous way to keep busy. Remember: an idle mind is the devil's workshop.

Anyway, here's my list of "Fun Facts about the Catholic Church."

The first thirty-five popes are saints. The first pope who didn't make the grade was Liberius. The next thirteen popes are also saints. Pope Anastatius II was the next pope not to make the grade. So out of the first 50 popes only two are not saints. Why did these two guys get stiffed? Well they both got caught in the middle of controversies—Liberius got caught in the crossfire over the Arian heresy and ironically got into trouble with the Roman Emperor Constantius II for standing up for orthodoxy. Anastatius II got embroiled in a schism and was viewed as a traitor to the church. Dante even put the poor guy in hell.

Another papal factoid: I feel compelled to report that the forty-sixth pope was St. Hilarius. Sometimes he's referred to as St. Hilary, but I'm not sure that helps.

"Stylites" were an ascetic sect in the fifth century who preached and incredibly, in some cases lived on pillars. St. Simeon Stylites the

Elder got up on a pillar somewhere in Syria in 423 and stayed there until he died 37 years later.

The concept of Seven Deadly Sins developed through the early church. In 590 Pope Gregory I organized the sins into the group we are familiar with today, i.e., lust, gluttony, greed, sloth, wrath, envy and pride.

In 897 Pope Stephen VI put on trial the corpse of Pope Formosus. Referred to as the Cadaver Synod, the trial was held in the Basilica of St. John Lateran in Rome. Stephen found the corpse of Formosus guilty of violations of canon law and perjury. He punished the corpse by stripping it of the papal vestments it was wearing and cutting off three of its fingers. The corpse was then reburied, but it was subsequently exhumed again and thrown into the Tiber River. These bizarre antics turned public opinion against Stephen. You think? He was eventually imprisoned, where he was strangled to death.

St. Francis of Assisi, famous for his acts of self-mortification and for receiving the stigmata, referred to his body as "Brother Ass."

When he went to school, Thomas Aquinas was known as "the Dumb Ox," even though he ended up being maybe the smartest guy in the entire thirteenth century.

In 1302, Pope Boniface VIII issued the papal bull, *Unum Sanctum.* In the bull the pope spoke *ex cathedra* and proclaimed that "outside" the church "there is neither salvation nor the remission of sins."

Similarly, in 1441, Pope Eugene IV, speaking *ex cathedra* in the papal bull *Cantate Domino*, stated that the church "firmly believes, professes, and proclaims that those not living within the Catholic Church, not only pagans, but also Jews and heretics and schismatics cannot become participants in eternal life, but will depart 'into everlasting fire which was prepared for the devil and his angels.'" (Matthew 25:41)

In 1428 Pope Martin V had the body of John Wycliffe, a Protestant reformer, dug up and burned at the stake.

In 1517 Martin Luther got bent out of shape over the issue of the church selling indulgences and wrote *Ninety-Five Theses*, attacking this practice and questioning the authority of the pope. He posted the document on the door of All Saints' Church in Wittenberg, Saxony, thereby starting the Protestant Reformation.

My favorite of the 95 theses is number 28: "It is certain that when the penny jingles into the money-box, gain and avarice can be increased, but the result of the intercession of the Church is in the power of God alone."

In case you didn't know, the official list of Catholic saints and beati is called the Roman Martyrology. It's called this even though obviously not every saint is a martyr, although there are a lot of them.

In 1854, Pope Pius IX, issued a decree, known as an Apostolic Constitution, titled *Ineffabilis Deus*. In the decree, speaking *ex cathedra,* he proclaimed the doctrine of the Immaculate Conception, i.e., that Mary the Mother of Jesus was conceived without original sin.

In 1870 the First Vatican Council decided that the Pope is infallible. The decision was also retroactive. The pope had always been infallible. The Catholic Church just waited almost 1,900 years to give everybody the scoop. If the idea of infallibility is kind of concerning, don't worry. The church says that the pope is not infallible on everything. He's only infallible when he says he is, and he promises that he will only say he is on matters of faith and morals. That's when he speaks *ex cathedra.* I don't know about you, but that makes me feel a whole lot better. It would make me kind of nervous if the pope suddenly decided to speak infallibly on String Theory or who should be the next Celebrity Apprentice.

In 1904 the Supreme Sacred Congregation of the Roman and Universal Inquisition became the Supreme Sacred Congregation of the

Holy Office. Then in 1965 it became the Sacred Congregation for the Doctrine of the Faith. That's sort of like Philip Morris Companies Inc. becoming the Altria Group.

If you write a book and you want to get an *imprimatur* from the church, i.e., the church's seal of approval, you first have to submit the book to a *Censor Librorum*, a "censor of books." The censor decides if your book contains anything that is contrary to church doctrine or damaging to faith and morals. If he finds nothing of the kind, he gives your book a *nihil obstat*, which means that "nothing hinders" it from being published. Then a bishop reviews the book and if the bishop agrees that there is no problem, you get your *imprimatur*. In case you're wondering, after a lot of soul searching, I decided not to submit *Papal Bull* to a *Censor Librorum*.

In 1941 at the age of fourteen, Joseph Ratzinger joined the Hitler Youth.

In 1962 Pope John XXIII excommunicated Fidel Castro.

In 1968 Pope Paul VI issued the encyclical, *Humanae Vitae*, re-affirming the church's teaching that all forms of contraception are immoral and contrary to natural law. Subsequently, the release of internal documents of the church commission that worked on the issue on behalf of the pope shows that there was significant support among commission members, which included Catholic theologians and bishops, for the use of contraception. According to these commission members, the use of contraception was neither immoral nor contrary to natural law.

Despite the church's teaching against contraception almost all Catholic women have at one point or another used some form of birth control, and a large majority of Catholic women who are sexually active and who do not want to become pregnant practice contraception.

In 1969, Pope Paul VI removed dozens of saints from the official church calendar either because they never existed or nothing was known about them.

In 1979 Mother Teresa was awarded the Nobel Peace Prize. In her acceptance speech she proclaimed that "the greatest destroyer of peace today is abortion."

In 1985 the Sacred Congregation for the Doctrine of the Faith dropped the term "Sacred" from its name.

Because of his aggressive style while serving as the Prefect of the Congregation for the Doctrine of the Faith, Cardinal Joseph Ratzinger, was dubbed "God's Rottweiler."

In 2000 the Congregation for the Doctrine of the Faith issued the declaration *Dominus Iesus: On the Unicity and Salvific Universality of Jesus Christ and the Catholic Church*, which reiterated the doctrine that the Roman Catholic Church is the one, true church, that other religions are inferior to Catholicism and that at best they offer an imperfect path to salvation.

How's this for a title? In 2005 the church published a document called *Instruction Concerning the Criteria for the Discernment of Vocations with regard to Persons with Homosexual Tendencies in view of their Admission to the Seminary and to Holy Orders.*

Pope John Paul II practiced self-flagellation, i.e., beating himself with a belt, to emulate the sufferings of Christ. If you think that maybe the source of this information had it in for John Paul, you'd be wrong. It appears in a book called *Why He Is a Saint,: The Life and Faith of Pope John Paul II and the Case for Canonization* written by Monsignor Slawomir Oder. He's a Polish priest who is the postulator for the canonization of John Paul, i.e., the guy appointed by the Vatican to build the case for sainthood.

Speaking of sainthood—during the papacy of Pope John Paul II there were 482 beatifications and 1,338 canonizations. That's more than all previous papacies combined.

In 2009 Benedict XVI reversed the excommunication of Richard Williamson, a bishop who denies the Holocaust. To be clear, Williamson's views on the Holocaust were not the reason for his excommunication in the first place. He was excommunicated because he had been made a bishop without the consent of the pope.

In April 2012 Pope Benedict XVI reprimanded American nuns for being too concerned with helping the poor. The pope wanted nuns to spend less time helping poor people and more time telling everybody that abortion and marriage equality are bad.

In June 2012 the Vatican censured Sister Margaret A. Farley's book, *Just Love: A Framework for Christian Sexual Ethics* six years after it was published. The book supports same-sex relationships, marriage equality and remarriage after divorce as well as arguing that masturbation does not pose any moral issues and may well help women discover "their own possibilities for pleasure."

In February 2013 Pope Benedict XV! resigned as pope. He was the first pope to resign since Pope Gregory XI in 1415 and is now known as Pope Emeritus. He was replaced by Cardinal Jorge Mario Bergoglio of Argentina, who took the name, Pope Francis.

In April 2013 Pope Francis reaffirmed the reprimand of American nuns that had been issued by his predecessor.

You usually have to perform two miracles from beyond the grave to become a saint. In July 2013 Pope Francis decided that Blessed Pope John Paul II had performed his second miracle—curing a woman of a brain aneurism—and was ready to be named a saint. However, in the same announcement, Pope Francis also decided that Pope John XXIII didn't need a second miracle and should be canonized anyway. Apparently the special waiver had something to do with the fact that the year 2013 is the 50th anniversary of Vatican II and also that Pope John was such a good guy.

You Don't Say!

There are just so many great things that the church has said over the past 2,000 years. I'm sure we all have our favorite quotes. Here are some of mine:

Our virgins are better than your virgins:

The comeliness of virginity never existed amongst the heathen, neither with the vestal virgins, nor amongst philosophers, such as Pythagoras. . . . How much stronger are our virgins, who overcome even those powers which they do not see; whose victory is not only over flesh and blood, but also over the prince of this world, and ruler of this age! —St. Ambrose, *Concerning Virginity*, Chapter 4.

If your baby has just died, comfort yourself by thinking that it's all for the best (because if he had lived, he might have turned into a really bad person, and if you don't believe that, just tell yourself that it's still the best possible outcome that he's dead because God never makes a mistake):

It is not unreasonable to conjecture that they would have plunged into a vicious life with a more desperate vehemence than any of those who have actually become notorious for their wickedness. That nothing happens without God we know from many sources; and, reversely, that God's dispensations have no element of chance and confusion in them every one will allow, who realizes that God is Reason, and Wisdom, and Perfect Goodness, and Truth, and could not admit of that which is not good and not consistent with His Truth. Whether, then, the early deaths of infants are to be attributed to the aforesaid causes, or whether there is some further cause of them beyond these, it befits us to acknowledge that these things happen for the best. —St. Gregory of Nyssa, *On Infants' Early Deaths.*

Be glad that you are miserable:

"The more we are afflicted in this world, the greater is our assurance in the next; the more sorrow in the present, the greater will be our joy in the future." —St. Isidore of Seville.
www.catholicbible101.com/quotesfromthesaints.htm.

Similarly, no matter how bad your life is, accept it, because it's all good:

We are at Jesus' disposal. If he wants you to be sick in bed, if he wants you to proclaim His work in the street, if he wants you to clean the toilets all day, that's all right, everything is all right. —Blessed Mother Teresa.
www.quotecatholic.com/index.php/category/happiness-joy/

I mean it, really. It's all good:

God takes an interest in the world and in all things created by Him; He preserves them, and governs them by His infinite goodness and wisdom; and nothing happens here below that He does not either will or permit. . . . there are some things which God wills and commands, while there are others which He simply does not prevent, such as sin. . . . God does not prevent sin, because even from the very abuse that man makes of the liberty with which he is endowed, God knows how to bring forth good and to make His mercy or His justice become more and more resplendent. —Pope St. Pius X, *The Catechism of Saint. Pius X.*

Suffering and self-mortification are necessary to salvation:

"Anyone who wants to be a true Christian . . . must mortify his flesh." —St. Padre Pio.

"I understood that to become a saint one had to suffer much." —St. Therese of Lisieux.

"I remind thee that there is no exercise more profitable and useful to the soul than to suffer." —Venerable Mary of Agreda.

"We love only to the degree that we are willing to suffer." —Fr. John A. Hardon, S.J.
www.religious-vocation.com/redemptive_suffering.html

If you're not a Catholic, you're going to hell:

"There is but one universal Church of the faithful outside of which no one at all is saved." —Pope Innocent III.

"We declare, say, define, and pronounce that it is absolutely necessary for the salvation of every human creature to be subject to the Roman Pontiff." —Pope Boniface VIII.

"Such is the nature of the Catholic faith that it does not admit of more or less, but must be held as a whole, or as a whole rejected: This is the Catholic faith, which unless a man believe faithfully and firmly, he cannot be saved." —Pope Benedict XV. http://www.bible.ca/cath-one-true-church.htm

In fact, it is wrong even to respect other peoples' religious beliefs:

The present emphasis placed on respecting other religions has contributed to indifferentism spreading like wildfire among the Catholic faithful. Indifferentism involves believing that one faith is as good as another and that all faiths merit salvation. . . . The only sound conclusion for all Roman Catholics is to respect only one religion, the True religion founded by Christ Himself: the Roman Catholic Church. To give esteem or regard to other false religions is to betray our Savior as Judas betrayed Him with thirty pieces of silver. —Edward D. Waller, Ph.D., "Respect for Other Religions?" *Catholic Family News*, August 1997.

Catholics who use contraceptives are no longer Catholic, are committing a mortal sin and are going to hell; even if you just advocate the use of contraception, you are no longer a Catholic (that means you, all you celibate or non-celibate liberal priests.):

The deliberate practice of contraception between husband and wife is objectively a mortal sin. . . . The grave sinfulness of contraception is taught infallibly by the Church's ordinary universal teaching authority. Therefore, those who defend contraception forfeit

their claim to being professed Catholics. —Fr. John A. Hardon. S.J., "Contraception: Fatal to the Faith."
www.hardonsj.org/article/2012/contraception-fatal-faith.

It's better to be celibate than to be married. (I might actually agree with the church on this point, although I would have to say that in many cases marriage and celibacy are one and the same thing):

"This doctrine of the excellence of virginity and of celibacy and of their superiority over the married state was . . . revealed by our Divine Redeemer." —Pope Pius XII.

"As a way of showing forth the Church's holiness, it is to be recognized that the consecrated life, which mirrors Christ's own way of life, **has an objective superiority**." —Blessed Pope John Paul II. www.religious-vocation.com.

It's just not manly to beat off—it's dirty too:

"By masturbating, i.e., 'by procuring pollution, without any copulation, for the sake of venereal pleasure; this pertains to the sin of 'uncleanness' which some call 'effeminacy.'" —Thomas Aquinas, Summa Theologica, II-II, Q. 154, Art. 11.

It's OK to be gay. You just can't ever have sex—actually it's not OK to be gay, and you can never have sex:

According to the teaching of the Church, men and women with homosexual tendencies 'must be accepted with respect, compassion and sensitivity. Every sign of unjust discrimination in their regard should be avoided.' They are called, like other Christians, to live the virtue of chastity. The homosexual inclination is however 'objectively disordered' and homosexual practices are 'sins gravely contrary to chastity.' —Cardinal Joseph Ratzinger, *Considerations Regarding Proposals to Give Legal Recognition to Unions between Homosexual Persons,* July 31, 2003

Laws protecting the right of gay people to marry are unjust:

In those situations where homosexual unions have been legally recognized or have been given the legal status and rights belonging to marriage, clear and emphatic opposition is a duty. One must refrain from any kind of formal cooperation in the enactment or application of such gravely unjust laws. —Cardinal Joseph Ratzinger, *Considerations Regarding Proposals to Give Legal Recognition to Unions between Homosexual Persons,* July 31, 2003.

It's good to be king, but it's even better to be the pope, especially if you have the following powers:

"That the Roman pontiff alone can with right be called universal."

"That of the pope alone all princes shall kiss the feet."

"That his name alone shall be spoken in the churches."

"That this is the only name in the world."

"That it may be permitted to him to depose emperors."

"That he himself may be judged by no one."

"That the Roman Church has never erred; nor will it to all eternity, the Scripture bearing witness." —Selections from *The Memorandum of the Pope,* Pope Gregory VII.

In conclusion, speaking of scripture:

"Blessed are the meek, for they shall inherit the earth." That would, of course, be from *The Sermon on the Mount.* It's one of the so-called Beatitudes. Maybe Pope Gregory missed that one.

THOSE WERE THE DAYS

Holy Wars

How can war be holy? Ask Blessed Pope Urban II or ask Osama bin Laden. Actually they're both dead, so you can't ask them (thank you, Barack Obama and Navy Seals for killing bin Laden), but when they were alive, they would have told you that a holy war is fought against infidels on behalf of the one true religion. Of course, these two guys were on different sides of the argument as to which religion is the one true religion, Christianity or Islam, but they totally agreed on the principles of holy war.

Although the idea of a holy war is implicit in Exodus in the God-sponsored genocide of the various peoples who got in the way of the Israelites occupying the Promised Land (i.e., they lived there), the idea of launching a Christian holy war against infidels appears to have been shaped most significantly by Pope Gregory VII, who was pope from 1073 to 1085. However, it was Pope Urban II who put Gregory's concepts into action a few years later. Gregory was the innovator; Urban was the chief marketing guy. If Urban's marketing plan were presented as a PowerPoint, what would the title be? How about "An Introduction to War Mongering"? Actually Urban pretty much nails the whole religious war-mongering thing. He presents a four-point plan. The cool thing is that even though it's intended to stir up Christians to fight Muslims, it's just as effective with slight modifications in stirring up Muslims against Christians or any religious group that might be incited to go to war against any other religious group. Here is Urban's four-point war-mongering plan:

1. Begin with a big lie. Tell everybody that the enemy you want to attack poses an immediate threat even though they don't.

2. Get everybody riled up about how they need to take back a holy city or shrine. Urban called on all Christians to take back Jerusalem from the Muslims as if they had just captured the city when in fact they had been there for more than four hundred years. To be precise, Urban articulated his marketing plan in 1095, and the Muslims took over Jerusalem in 638. I guess news really didn't travel very fast in those days.

3. Demonize your enemy. Accuse them of having committed every imaginable atrocity. Basically establish that they are sub-human and have no right to live.

4. Guarantee that participation in the holy war gives all participants a free pass to heaven. Just let everybody know that God sanctions the war, approves of any and all slaughter and that all of your sins will be forgiven if you fight in the war. In other words, make mass murder a path to salvation.

Urban's war-mongering plan is so good, you can even use parts of it to launch a secular war. For example, when George Bush, Dick Cheney and the Neocons made the case for why the US needed to go to war against Iraq, they certainly followed Urban's marketing plan by beginning with a big lie (weapons of mass destruction) and then bolstered the big lie with an even bigger lie that demonized the enemy (i.e., that Saddam Hussein was responsible for the 911 attacks). You could even say, with a bit of a stretch, that they used Urban's holy city of Jerusalem point too in the sense that they said that Iraq was a direct threat to Israel as well as the United States. So no doubt about it, Urban's war-mongering plan was great way back in the eleventh century, and it's still great today.

What was the immediate effect of Urban's plan? Well, Urban was looking for more than a few good men, and he did a whole lot better than that. He got more than a few good men, women and children. Estimates vary quite a bit, but it's clear that tens of thousands of men volunteered to go out and kill a whole bunch of people they had never even met, and these brave men were accompanied by several thousand women and children. Apparently, back then, a lot of people felt that genocidal slaughter was something that you should do together as a family—sort of like, the family that kills together stays together.

Actually the whole family values angle is just one of the things that people don't know about the Crusades. To be fair, they did get started almost a thousand years ago, so it's not entirely surprising that people are a little fuzzy on what the Crusades were really all about. They might have some vague idea about idealistic knights under the leadership of legendary kings like Richard the Lionheart and Louis IX protecting Christendom from the threat of Muslim occupation. In reality it was a series of totally unnecessary wars spanning about two hundred years in which people were killed because of their religion— Christians massacring Muslims; Muslims massacring Christians, and Christians slaughtering Jews as well. Here are a few highlights:

- Urban's call for a Crusade against Muslims incited a wave of violence against Jews. Even before the first Crusade was launched, there were massacres of Jews in France, Germany, Bohemia and Hungary.

- After an eight-month siege the crusaders gained entrance to the city of Antioch as a result of the betrayal of one of the tower commanders and proceeded to massacre virtually everyone in the city—not just Muslims but Christian Greeks, Syrians and Armenians as well.

- In 1099 starving crusaders cannibalized their Muslim victims in Marrat, Syria.

- After a long siege when the crusaders gained access to the city of Jerusalem, they perpetrated a citywide massacre of Muslims and Jews.

That brings us to the end of the first Crusade. There were eight more. What is there to say about those Crusades and a whole lot more religiously inspired military expeditions that just aren't counted as official Crusades? Crazy wars that went on for hundreds and hundreds of years: Etc. That's right. Etc. Just more of the same mindless slaughter. Just more of the same killing. Over and over again. Just one massacre after another.

Etc., etc., etc.

Enhanced Interrogation

I've been trying really hard, but I still can't find a single Cathar anywhere. I now realize that no matter how hard I try, I will never find a single Cathar. That's because there aren't any. In fact, they haven't been around for almost 700 years, so don't feel bad if you've never heard of them. Who were they? Well, the Cathars were people who belonged to a religious movement that flourished in France and Northern Italy from the second half of the twelfth century into the early part of the fourteenth century. The Cathars were dualists who believed that the presence of evil in the world meant that there had to be two Gods—a good God who created the spiritual world and a bad God who created the material world. The belief in a good God and a bad God goes back a long way and actually precedes Christianity. Of course, according to the Catholic Church, it is simply heresy, and heresy—also known as diversity of belief—has to be wiped out.

The Cathars were wiped out—completely. To be precise, they were "extirpated." That is the word that the church itself used to indicate its objective with respect to what it defined as heretical beliefs. To "extirpate" means to destroy completely down to the root. It's like what your landscaper does to crab grass. The Cathars were extirpated by a combination of the Albigensian Crusade, also known as the Cathar Crusade, which lasted almost half a century from 1209-1255, and the Inquisition, which officially kicked off in 1231 when Pope Gregory IX appointed the first group of inquisitors.

Now we know there is only one perfect mass murderer, and that is God. Forget about the story of Noah's Ark where God killed every single person on the face of the earth except Noah and his family. Never mind the much more modest genocidal slaughter of the people who lived in the Promised Land when it was time for the People of Israel to move in. God is the one who invented death. Death is his idea. So he eventually gets everybody. You can't possibly do better than that. That is a level of homicidal achievement that no one can ever come close to duplicating. But let me tell you something. Those Inquisition guys were good, particularly the Dominicans. They had a dedication to delivering their own Final Solution to heresy that could serve as a model for other mass murderers in the future—Hitler, Stalin, Mao—whoever. I know those guys were all atheists, but I think they would still give credit where credit is due and tip their hats to all of the popes and Inquisitors who dedicated themselves to the extirpation of heretics for so many years.

I like to give credit as well. So let me recognize here the Stars of the Inquisition. Disclaimer: The Inquisition went on for centuries in one form or another, so I know I'll be leaving out hundreds, maybe even thousands, of people who were deeply committed to stamping out the lives of people who had the temerity to express different beliefs. Apologies to all of you. But here in my estimation are the biggest Stars of the Inquisition, the truly legendary few who made the word "Inquisition" synonymous with terror and torture to this very day.

Pope Gregory IX: The church had always suppressed heresies ever since it was established as the state religion in the fourth century, but, as I mentioned above, it was Pope Gregory IX who got the Medieval Inquisition officially started when he formally appointed Inquisitors to combat heresy, thereby making them direct agents of the pope.

Pope Innocent IV: Gregory IX formally kicked off the inquisition, so he was in a sense the originator. Innocent IV, however, gets the credit for elevating the Inquisition to an almost mythic status in the history of totalitarian thought control and terror by issuing the papal bull *Ad Extirpanda*, which called for the extirpation of all heretics. As David Renaker points out in the introduction to his translation of *Ad Extirpanda*, Innocent brilliantly leaves heresy undefined so that anyone can be accused of it by the Inquisition. So-called heretics were actually found guilty of heresy before they were even publicly accused let alone tried. There was no chance for them to prove their innocence. Innocent also makes the identification of heretics an obligation of the head of state. Failure to comply with any of the 38 Inquisition laws set forth in *Ad Extirpanda* results not only in the head of state losing all authority but also in the country itself losing its status as a sovereign nation, thus leaving it open to invasion and confiscation of all of its territory.

Accused heretics immediately lost all of their property, were fined and arrested. Their homes were leveled to the ground and were never rebuilt. If you harbored a heretic in your home or in a building that you owned, the home or building was leveled as well as all of the other properties you owned. Indeed, anyone offering any defense of an accused heretic or petitioning for their release from prison lost all of their property as well. Most notably, in law 25 Innocent authorizes the use of torture against accused heretics. Specifically he states that "The head of state or ruler must force all the heretics whom he has in custody, provided he does so without killing them or breaking their arms or legs, as actual robbers and murderers of souls and thieves of the sacraments of God and Christian faith, to confess their errors and accuse other heretics whom they know, and specify their motives, and those whom they have seduced, and those who have lodged them and defended them, as thieves and robbers of material goods are made to accuse their accomplices and confess the crimes they have committed."

For authoring what amounts not only to the textbook for the Inquisition but the textbook for all totalitarian campaigns against freedom of thought, speech and religion, Innocent IV deserves recognition as one of the truly legendary Stars of the Inquisition.

Bernard Gui: A Dominican appointed as Inquisitor of Toulouse in 1307 by Pope Clement V. In this role he was instrumental in extirpating the Cathars. He was the author of *Practica Officii Inquisitionis Heretice Pravitatis* or "Conduct of the Inquisition into Heretical Wickedness," a how-to book for Inquisitors that provided guidance on such topics as how to conduct an interrogation and how to sentence a heretic to death. He was also the author of *Liber Sententiarum* the "Book of Sentences," a meticulously organized personal journal that recorded the details of his finding some 633 men and women guilty of heresy over a period of 15 years. The sentences varied. Some of the Jewish heretics were made to wear yellow crosses to identify them as Jews. In the case of some heretics who had already died, Gui had their corpses dug up and burned and their houses destroyed. On one particularly busy day, he condemned seventeen people to be burned at the stake.

Dominic Guzman (St. Dominic): Founder of the Dominican Order, the primary source from which the various Inquisition popes recruited their Inquisitors. Since he is honored as a saint, the church has attempted to distance Guzman from participation in the horrors of the Inquisition. For example, the *Catholic Encyclopedia* tries unsuccessfully to minimize his involvement by stating that "if he was for a certain time identified with the operations of the Inquisition, it was only in the capacity of a theologian passing upon the orthodoxy of the accused." This would mean quite obviously that Guzman was in some cases identifying who should be executed as a heretic. I'm not sure how selecting who should be executed is in any way exculpatory. Notwithstanding such lame attempts to whitewash his involvement, it is clear that Guzman led the Inquisition against the Cathars, which as I noted above, resulted in their complete extirpation. Furthermore, Bernard Gui himself identifies Guzman as an Inquisitor. Without a doubt, Dominic Guzman is one of the all time Inquisition All Stars.

Nicholas Eymerich: Like Gui, Eyermich was a Dominican, an Inquisitor and an author—his most famous work is *Directorium Inquisitorum*. Eymerich was an expert on interrogation techniques, a big proponent of torture and a big time Jew hater. He was also obsessed with the subject of sorcery as heresy. Yes, that's right. Sorcery. He wanted to catch, torture and kill people who were communicating with demons, making pacts with demons, worshipping demons, etc. Eymerich is a quintessential Inquisition All Star.

Jacques Fournier: Bishop of Pamiers, Inquisitor and later Pope Benedict XII. He personally conducted hundreds of interrogations and recorded these proceedings in great detail in what is known as the Fournier Register.

King Ferdinand II of Aragon and Queen Isabella of Castile: A lot of people think of King Ferdinand and Queen Isabella as the enlightened monarchs who backed Columbus on his voyages across the Atlantic to find a new route to the East Indies. Since the premise of Columbus's expeditions was that the world was round, not flat, the king and queen must have been fairly progressive for their time.

Right? Wrong. They just thought that if Columbus somehow found a new route to the East Indies, even if it was a really long shot, they could control the spice trade, so there was nothing enlightened about their support. It was all about power and greed. Meanwhile Ferdinand and Isabella are included here as All Stars of the Inquisition because they launched the Spanish Inquisition in 1478, with a particular focus on persecuting Jews. In fact, the anti-Semitism of the Inquisition came to a head in that famous year of 1492 when the king and queen issued the Edict of Expulsion, which ordered that all Jews had to leave Aragon and Castile within three months. Tens of thousands of Jews were forced to leave. Those who stayed had to convert to Christianity and ironically made themselves targets of the Inquisition, which challenged the authenticity of the Jewish converts. As a result, tens of thousands of these *conversos* were expelled from the country by the Inquisition. The Spanish Inquisition was particularly long-lived and was not formally abolished until 1834. Amazingly, the Edict of Expulsion had an even longer shelf life. It wasn't rescinded until 1968. That's quite a legacy for the good king and queen.

Tomás de Torquemada: Another Dominican, the confessor of Queen Isabella and the most notorious Inquisitor of the Spanish Inquisition. In fact, he was Grand Inquisitor from 1483 until his death in 1498, and he certainly earned the name. He dramatically expanded the scope of the Inquisition beyond Seville into numerous cities and towns throughout Spain and relentlessly persecuted Jews and Muslims who had been forced to convert to Christianity, accusing them of being false converts. Torquemada had his own Inquisition manual, called *Compilación de las Instruciones del Oficio de la Santa Inquisición.* He was a fierce advocate of torture in the case of accused heretics who refused to confess, particularly employing such techniques as suspension or reverse hanging, the rack and the *toca* or water cloth—what is currently known as waterboarding. Exact numbers of victim's are hard to know, but during Torquemada's fifteen-year tenure as Grand Inquisitor tens of thousands of people were prosecuted. Certainly hundreds and perhaps as many as 2,000 people were burned at the stake.

Pope Urban VIII: Originally a friend and patron of Galileo Galilei. However, when Galileo was preparing his book, *Dialogue Concerning the Two Chief World Systems*, in which he would discuss the competing heliocentric and geocentric views, Urban asked that his own geocentric views be included in the book. Galileo did so but put them in the mouth of a character named Simplicio. This did not go over well with the pope. Subsequently Galileo went on trial before the Roman Inquisition for asserting that the earth revolved around the sun. He recanted this view but was forced by the inquisition to live the rest of his life under house arrest.

Editors of the *Catholic Encyclopedia*: These guys receive special recognition as honorary All Stars of the Inquisition. Writing and editing at the beginning of the twentieth century, almost 700 hundred years after the Inquisition was officially launched, the CE editors totally support the idea that it is God's work to suppress heresy. "Moderns"—the rather odd word the editors use to describe their educated and humane contemporaries—just don't understand. "Religious belief" is "objective," a "gift of God," lying "outside the realm of free private judgment." Translation: The Catholic Church is the one, true church, and no one has the right to any other religious belief. All other religious beliefs are heresy and must be extirpated by any means necessary. Torture? The CE editors have no problem with it whatsoever so long as the torturers follow the papal guidelines: apply torture once (whatever that means) and make sure the subject of the torture does not lose an arm, a leg or die. Indeed, according to the editors, "Had this papal legislation been adhered to in practice, the historian of the Inquisition would have fewer difficulties to satisfy." Wow! Talk about retro. You cannot possibly be more retro than being pro-Inquisition— and these guys pull it off without breaking a sweat. Editors of the *Catholic Encyclopedia*—you wannabe Inquisitor guys—I salute you! You are truly All Stars of the Inquisition.

Postscript to Enhanced Interrogation: Talk about a War on Women! A particularly ugly and barbaric aspect of the inquisition was the persecution of women as witches. In 1487, two Inquisitors, Heinrich Kramer and James Sprenger, published the notorious *Malleus Maleficarum* ("The Hammer of Witches"). The book claims that witches gain power through having sex with the devil and describes how they practice their evil craft. It also provides detailed instructions on how to prosecute witches. Witch-hunts were not limited to the Inquisition, of course. They were conducted by various Catholic, Protestant and secular authorities, with peak activity extending from the fifteenth to the eighteenth centuries. Tens of thousands of people, overwhelmingly women, were executed, usually by burning or hanging.

CANONIZATION

What Is a Saint?

You would think that it would be pretty easy to say what a saint is. Isn't a saint a really holy person who deserves to be honored? Isn't that it? Well, maybe not. Actually, if you look at the total population of saints from the beginning of the church, you get a whole different picture.

First of all, how many saints are there? Apparently nobody knows, not even the Catholic Church. There does not seem to be any definitive count. According to www.catholic.org "there are over 10,000 named saints and beati," (i.e., individuals who have been beatified, which is a step toward formally becoming a saint), but "there is no definitive 'head count.'"

Now you would think that at the very least you would actually have to exist to become a saint. I for one think that should be the minimum requirement. But apparently I am wrong. Lots of saints never existed, as I mentioned in "Fun Facts." In 1969 the church purged a whole bunch of saints, taking their names off of the liturgical calendar either because they never existed or because there was no reliable information about them and no way to be sure that they did exist. It must have been pretty embarrassing for the church to admit that for centuries it had been venerating as saints people who never existed, especially since the church almost never admits that it's wrong. But in this case the church did—well, sort of.

One of the saints that the church removed from the calendar

because he never existed was St. Valentine. That's amazing since St. Valentine has to be one of the most popular saints of all time. After all, Valentine's Day is beloved by lovers all over the world. Well, here's the surprise. Even though the church removed him from the calendar, St. Valentine is still a saint! He is still on the official saint list, which was most recently revised in 2005. So in fact you do not have to exist in order to be a saint. St. Christopher is still a saint too even though he was removed from the calendar because we know absolutely nothing about him and he probably didn't exist. Maybe he got the benefit of the doubt because of how many Saint Christopher medals have been sold.

Now, one more question. Do you have to be holy to be a saint? Or to put it plainly, do you even have to be a good person? Once again, you would think that being good was a requirement for being a saint, but it turns out that this isn't true either. Now an objection that a lot of people seem to have about condemning behavior from centuries ago is that it's anachronistic and that you have to cut these people a lot of slack because they were products of their benighted and ignorant times. However, I'm going to go out on a limb anyway and say I think things like hating women, hating Jews, burning down libraries or destroying the culture and art of other people, inciting mobs to kill people, torturing people, or committing mass murder or genocide were always really bad. Also, we're not talking about whether or not these people reflected the views of their time. We're talking about whether they deserve to be honored as saints. I would think that saying that somebody was no better than the barbaric times they were living in would definitely mean that they weren't a saint. Doesn't being a saint require that you exhibit moral leadership and rise above the prevailing prejudices and ignorance of your times? Moreover, isn't being a saint different from being the most prominent theologian of your time or a great translator of the Bible or a great preacher?

If you take the position that saints should not say and do incredibly evil things and be better than their times, you have some major issues. Some of the most famous saints would have to be removed from the saint list. I'll just name a few of them, along with a few "beati," and provide some sample quotes or explanatory notes. Sorry if some saints appear in multiple categories:

Saints who denigrated women: Oops! We start with a bit of a dilemma. Since the Catholic Church itself denigrates and discriminates against women, you have to expect that denigrating and discriminating against women is not going to disqualify you from becoming a saint. Actually you would really have to include here just about every single male saint and a lot of female saints since they embraced the church's teaching on the inferiority and subordination of women and on the supposed divine injunction against ordaining women, so on this point I recommend that you just go back to "Where Are the Women?" if you want to treat yourself a second time to some astonishingly misogynistic remarks from some of the most prominent saints in the Catholic Church.

Saints who made hateful statements about Jews: Making hateful statements is a pretty good indication of actual hatred, so even though we can't read their minds, these saints are condemned as anti-Semites by their own words. (Note: Christian hatred of Jewish people is based in part on the insane idea that all Jews are responsible for the death of Jesus, who was of course Jewish. This idea was particularly popular among the early Fathers of the Church. When you think of it, this is really a variation on the idea of original sin.) To name just a few anti-Semitic saints: St. Justin Martyr, St. Irenaeus, St. Cyprian, St. Clement, St. Jerome, St. Ambrose, St. Gregory of Nyssa, St. Augustine, St. John

Chrysostom, St. Hyppolytus, St. Cyril of Alexandria, Pope St. Pius V.

A few quotes provide a good idea of what I'm talking about:

St. John Chrysostom: In *Eight Homilies Against the Jews*—yes, that's what it's called—he says, "Although such beasts are unfit for work, they are fit for killing. And this is what happened to the Jews: while they were making themselves unfit for work, they grew fit for slaughter." (Homily I, II) Also: "The synagogue is not only a brothel . . . it is also a den of robbers and a lodging for wild beasts." (Homily I, III) Also: Jews "live for their bellies, they gape for the things of this world, their condition is not better than that of pigs or goats because of their wanton ways and excessive gluttony." (Homily I, IV) One more: "Isaiah called the Jews dogs and Jeremiah called them mare-mad horses. This was not because they suddenly changed natures with those beasts but because they were pursuing the lustful habits of those animals." (Homily IV, Vi, 3)

St. Hippolytus: *Expository Treatise Against the Jews*: "Now, then, incline your ear to me, and hear my words, and give heed, you Jew. Many a time do you boast yourself, in that you condemned Jesus of Nazareth to death, and gave Him vinegar and gall to drink; and you vaunt yourself because of this. Come therefore, and let us consider together whether perchance you do not boast unrighteously, O Israel, (and) whether that small portion of vinegar and gall has not brought down this fearful threatening upon you, (and) whether this is not the cause of your present condition involved in these myriad troubles."

The Catholic Church has venerated as saints a number of children whom it has claimed without any evidence were ritually murdered by Jews. These include St. William of Norwich, Little St. Hugh of Lincoln,

St. Simon of Trent and St. Christopher of Toledo. There is an entirely fictional account, drenched in anti-Semitism, in the *Lives of the Saints* of the murder of Simon. The description is deeply unsettling, betraying a pathological and strangely pornographic fascination with the imagined details of the killing. An anti-Semitic cult has grown up around the murdered child.

Saints who led or supported movements to torture and kill people, like the Inquisition, or who led or supported movements promoting mass murder and genocide, like the Crusades:

Inquisition: St. Dominic, St. Peter of Verona, St. Francis of Assisi, St. James of the Marches, St. John Capistran.

Crusades:

- Blessed Pope Urban II: He only made it to "blessed," but I'm including him anyway because he launched the first Crusade.

- Blessed Pope Eugene III: I'll include him too because he launched the second Crusade.

- St. Louis (King Louis IX): Led the seventh and eighth Crusades.

Now that's some pretty nasty stuff coming from a bunch of guys who are among the biggest saints in the Catholic Church. You hate women, hate Jews, torture people, kill people—and you're a saint. How's that? Well, maybe we should just think of the Catholic Church as being like major league baseball and then think of being named a saint in the same way that we think of baseball players getting elected to the Hall of Fame. Some of them may have been pretty bad guys—like Cap Anson and Ty Cobb—but boy did they ever know how to play ball.

Patron Saints

A patron saint is somebody you pray to for a specific reason. For example, if you lose something, you pray to St. Anthony to find it because he's the patron saint of lost things. He achieved this distinction because one day he realized his prayer book was missing and after praying to get it back, he somehow appeared to the woman who had borrowed it, which of course scared the crap out of her, and she gave him back the book right away. I don't think it's supposed to be a joke, but St. Anthony is also the patron saint of amputees.

Here's a very brief list of some more patron saints. I'm sorry I don't have an explanation for every one. I don't think the Catholic Church does either.

St. Elmo—*Abdominal pains:* This is because he supposedly was tortured by having hot iron hooks stuck into his stomach, but he miraculously recovered. Actually Elmo is quite a versatile patron saint. He's the St. Elmo of "St. Elmo's Fire," i.e., the blue light that sometimes appears around ships and is seen as a sign of protection. They sort of look like explosions, so Elmo's also the patron saint of explosives workers—they're the "Hurt Locker" guys.

St. Jude—*Impossible causes:* Mets fans, he's for you.

St. Hillary of Poitiers—*Backward children:* I have no explanation for this. Actually I'm wondering more what the Catholic Church's definition is of a "backward child" than why Hillary is their patron saint.

St. Benedict the Black—*Black people:* No comment. (On second thought, I should say that there is no patron saint of white people. Apparently they don't need one.)

St. Clare of Assisi—*Television:* This is because she was too sick to go to Mass on Christmas Day one year, but because of a miracle she was able to see and hear the Mass anyway from her bed.

St. Joseph of Arimathea—*Funeral directors:* That's because he claimed the body of Jesus after he was crucified. He's also the patron saint of gravediggers.

St. Joseph of Cupertino—*Pilots and air travelers:* Joseph has to share this distinction with Our Lady of Loreto. I'm sure he doesn't mind. If you'd like to know why he is the patron saint of pilots and air travelers, I can tell you—he was able to fly. That's right. Isn't that amazing? I wonder if he was also the inspiration for "The Flying Nun," the 1960s TV show that literally launched the career of Sally Field

St. Joseph, i.e., the St. Joseph, the foster father of Jesus—*Happy Death:* Now there's an oxymoron. I guess it's because we assume that when he died, Jesus and Mary were there with him.

St. Bonaventure—*Bowel disorders:* I'll be praying to him before my next colonoscopy.

St. Anthony the Abbott—*Pigs:* I don't want to know why.

St. Dymphna—*Insanity:* Leave it to the church to give insane people a patron saint no one's ever heard of.

St. John Francis Regis—*illegitimate children:* Message to the church: there are no illegitimate children.

The Madonna of Castallazzo—*Bikers.*

St. Drogo—*Mute people:* He is also the patron saint of sheep. I hope that doesn't offend the mute people.

St. Raphael, the Archangel—*Obsessive Compulsive Disorder.*

St. George—*Herpes:* I assume that covers both cold sores and genital herpes, but I wonder if it includes chicken pox and shingles too. I don't think there's anybody to pray to about HPV. You just have to see your doctor.

St. Mary Magdalene—*Reformed prostitutes* and *hairdressers:* Does that mean that a lot of reformed prostitutes become hairdressers?

St. Vitus—*Comedians:* I think he was the first standup.

Note: There is apparently no patron saint of atheists. There is also no patron saint of gay or transgender people. Oh well, maybe some day.

It's Gonna Take a Miracle

I sort of wish the Catholic Church would go back to its old way of picking saints—the way they did it back in the day, back when the church first started. Basically, if the church felt like making you a saint, you were a saint. There was no process. It was just a popularity contest—even a pope-ularity contest. As I note in "Fun Facts," the first 35 popes are saints. They couldn't all be that good. They were just very connected—don't you think? As I've also pointed out, you didn't even have to exist to be a saint, so if somebody important just liked the idea of you, you could be a saint—like St. Valentine or St. Ursula (her 11,000 virgins aren't saints, but I think that Ursula would have acknowledged them in her acceptance speech, if she had existed.).

Anyway, the church now has a very formal and elaborate canonization process. That's what they call making somebody a saint—canonizing them. It sounds painful to be canonized, like you would at least need to be under local anesthesia—but maybe I'm thinking of "cauterized." Whatever. It really is just the word they use to describe how they vet saints, and I'm sure it does a good job of at least weeding out candidates that never existed. Here's the problem, though. Once the church has decided that you are worthy of being considered for sainthood by having led a life of what it calls "heroic virtue," the main requirement for actually becoming a saint is that you have to perform or somehow take credit for making miracles happen from beyond the grave. In fact, the church says that it doesn't really name saints. God does. According to the church, the dead saint performing miracles is God's way of letting everybody know the would-be saint is in heaven and he and the saint are as close as white on rice. How convenient! So once the pope canonizes a saint, that decision has to be infallible because God is really making the decision, and he has never made a mistake with the possible exception of when he created the world in the first place.

Let's take a look at the two dead people who are far and away the most famous candidates currently under consideration for sainthood—Mother Teresa and Pope John Paul II. There's a nice connection here because before he died John Paul II waived the five-year waiting period for Mother Teresa. He totally fast-tracked her candidacy and she made it to "blessed" in record time. That's because a woman in India, who is described as non-Christian, went to bed one night with a gigantic stomach tumor and when she woke up, it was all gone. That's because the nuns who used to work for Mother Teresa were praying to Mother Teresa to make the tumor disappear, and it did. But that's not all. Mother Teresa made the tumor disappear on the first anniversary of her death. Talk about being tight with God. That really takes the cake! On the basis of this truly impressive and timely miracle Pope John Paul II beatified Mother Teresa.

Now what about John Paul II? As you might expect, he is really on the fast track. His successor, Pope Benedict XVI, waived the five-year waiting period for him, too. He wasn't going to let anything get in the way of speeding along the sainthood train for John Paul II—certainly not the church's child sex abuse scandal. After all, John Paul II was such a great pope and such a great man that it just doesn't matter that he allowed rapists and abusers along with the priests and bishops who protected them to stay in their positions of power and in fact did everything he could to delay and obstruct the investigation into the abuse.

In 2011 Benedict XVI beatified John Paul II. It turns out a French nun was cured of Parkinson's disease after her nun friends prayed to John Paul II. She was supposedly cured of the disease one night after she wrote down the pope's name on a piece of paper. What a miracle! Especially when you take into account that Parkinson's is the very disease that John Paul II suffered from himself. I'm sure that made him feel a very special empathy for the poor sick nun.

Back to my original point—I think the guys back in the good old days of the church had it right. If they wanted to make somebody a saint, they just did it. They knew they had the power. Why mess around? It's hard to laugh at a church that doesn't blink when it makes anti-Semites, misogynists, torturers and mass murderers saints. It's hard not to laugh at a church that bases sainthood on disappearing stomach tumors and phantom cures.

PONTIFICATION

The Pope Awards

There have been 266 popes in more than 2,000 years. As you might imagine, it's very hard to stand out in that kind of crowd. I'd like to recognize a few popes who have managed to do just that—stand out from the crowd and do it in their own unique ways. Even if their achievements are sometimes dubious, they still make us sit up and take notice, and that is worth something. So to them and to the indelible marks they have made upon history, I dedicate the "Pope Awards":

Most Innovative Use of the Vatican: This award goes to John XII. According to contemporary accounts, he turned the Lateran Palace, i.e., the papal residence, into a whorehouse. Those were the days!

Youngest pope: Hey, John XII wins this award too! He was eighteen when he became pope. How did he do that? Well, his father was Alberic II, the ruler of Rome.

Like Father, Like Son—the Nepotism Award: Stiff competition here—for centuries being named pope was all about family ties. In fact, the word "nepotism" derives from the practice during the Middle Ages of popes making their nephews cardinals. Despite all of the competition, I think this award goes to the father and son team of Anastasius I and Innocent I. Innocent, the son, succeeded his father, Anastatius, as pope. Not only that, they're both saints. Way to go guys!

Most Outrageous Party Thrown by a Pope and His Children: Unlike a lot of the other awards, there is a clear winner in this category if the story is true. The party was recorded by Johann Burchard, the Papal Master of Ceremonies, in his chronicle of papal ceremonies, entitled *Liber Notarum*. It is known as the Ballet of the Chestnuts. According to Burchard, it was held in the Papal Palace in 1501, and was attended by Alexander VI, aka Rodrigo Borgia; his son, Cardinal Cesare Borgia; and his daughter, Lucrezia. Also in attendance were fifty prostitutes. After dinner, the prostitutes danced naked. Chestnuts were strewn about the floor, and the prostitutes had to pick up the chestnuts as they crawled about. At the ensuing orgy, prizes were given to the guests who put on the best sexual performances with the prostitutes. A Vatican researcher has disputed the authenticity of the story, but, considering the well-documented depravity of the Borgias, they must certainly be given the benefit of the doubt and with it the award for the most outrageous family gathering in papal history.

Be Fruitful and Multiply: This award goes to the pope with the most children. Hard to know the true numbers here, but we know Alexander VI had at least seven children, (I've seen estimates of as many as eleven), so I'm giving the award to him.

Now That's Crazy: This award is for the single craziest act ever committed by a pope. Once again, there's a lot of competition, but I think I have a clear-cut winner. I've already mentioned this in fun facts, but I have to give this award to Stephen VI for digging up the dead body of his predecessor, Pope Formosus and putting the corpse on trial.

Meanest: Again, an embarrassment of riches, but I'm going with Urban VI. He had a number of cardinals arrested and tortured for conspiring against him. While they were being tortured, Urban walked about his garden and read from his prayer book—all the while listening to the screams of the cardinals.

Best Quote: Attributed to Leo X—"Since God has given us the papacy, let us enjoy it." Even if he didn't actually say it, he certainly lived by it.

Most Entrepreneurial: There were so many popes who were wheeler-dealers, but you just can't beat Benedict IX. Forget selling indulgences, he actually sold the papacy itself. No way you can top that. The nephew of the two previous popes, Benedict became pope in 1032 but was deposed by Sylvester III in 1044. He regained the papacy by force a year later but almost immediately sold it to his godfather, Gregory VI.

Three Strikes and You're Out: This award also goes to Benedict IX. In 1046 a synod formally deposed him, his godfather and Sylvester, and Henry III, the king of Germany, appointed a new pope, Clement II. When Clement died the next year, Benedict jumped in again and became pope for the third time. He was kicked out again the following year. Nevertheless, Benedict does enjoy the distinction of being the only person to serve three discontinuous terms as pope.

The Original Godfather: Mario Puzo, the author of *The Godfather*, called the Borgias the first crime family. That would make Alexander VI the first Godfather. Alex wins again!

Love and Death: A four-way tie: John VII and John XII were reportedly killed by their mistress's husbands while they were *in flagrante delicto*. An alternative version of John XII's death has him suffering a stroke while having sex and dying a week later. Either way he gets a share of the award (that's three awards, tying him with Alexander VI for the most.) Leo VII reportedly died of a heart attack while having sex, and then there's my favorite love and death story—Pope Paul II died while being sodomized by a page boy. The story is alleged, not confirmed. Absurdly, the official cause of death was from a heart attack after suffering indigestion from eating a melon. Who gets indigestion from eating a melon? Anyway, the sodomy story is just too good to ignore, so Paul gets a share of the award.

Top Torturer: Pope Innocent IV for making the Papal Inquisition legendary.

Top Jihadist: Pope Urban II wins for launching the first Crusade in 1095.

Look the Other Way: I'm sorry, but I have to call this one a draw. The "Look the Other Way" Pope Award goes to Pope Pius XII for never once saying or doing anything to oppose the Holocaust and to Blessed Pope John Paul II for obstructing the investigation into the church's sexual abuse scandal. I hate not picking a clear-cut winner, but I'm afraid this one is a dead heat. Of course, obstruction is more than just looking the other way, so Pope John Paul II committed more than just a sin of omission. But I'm still calling this one a tie.

The Anti-Pope Awards

You don't hear much about the anti-popes. They just don't get a lot of love. But there were several dozen of them—37 to be exact. Anti-popes were guys who opposed the elected pope and said they should be pope instead. The first anti-pope was Anti-Pope St. Hippolytus in 217. The last one was Anti-Pope Amadeus of Savoy in 1449. So these anti-pope guys were around off and on for more than 1,200 years. How's that for not taking no for an answer? I just gave out a bunch of Pope Awards. I think the anti-popes deserve awards too, so here goes.

Saintliest Anti-Pope: This award has to go to Anti-Pope St. Hippolytus because he's the only anti-pope who is also a saint. I'm still trying to figure out exactly how he got to be a saint because he was, hello, an anti-pope, not a pope, and he ended up getting exiled to Sardinia for supporting a schism or maybe because everybody just got sick of his anti-poping. So how the heck did he become a saint? Well, I have a few theories on this. Here they are:

- In those days every single pope became a saint. As I point out in "What Is a Saint?" The first 35 popes were saints, so maybe the saint makers back then felt bad about the idea of leaving out Hippolytus, and they decided to make him a saint too even though he was an anti-pope and not the real pope. In fact, he actually opposed four popes in a row, which is why maybe people eventually got sick of him and exiled him to Sardinia. Another thought: Maybe some of the saint-making guys thought Hippolytus should have really been the pope at least one of the four times that he was the anti-pope. That's possible, maybe even likely. I mean, think of all of the people, including me, who believe Al Gore actually won the 2000 presidential election even though he officially lost by one vote.

- Hippolytus was very persistent in his anti-poping. I just mentioned that he opposed four popes in a row. They were Pope St. Callistus I, Pope St. Urban I, Pope St. Pontain and Pope St. Anterus. I sort of think of Hippolytus as the Ron Paul of the early church. Or maybe Harold Stassen, if anybody remembers him. Maybe Hippolytus's incredible persistence helped him to be named a saint, even if it also annoyed lots of people.

- Hippolytus was a big-time Jew hater, and I'm sure this won him a lot of points and was a big factor in making him a saint. Hippolytus's *Expository Treatise Against the Jews* is a Jew-hating classic even though only part of the original text has survived. You can read every single Jew-hating word that did survive by going to www.newadvent.com. That would, of course, be the website of the *Catholic Encyclopedia*.

- Hippolytus was thought to be a martyr, and he's still listed as a martyr, even though he wasn't. Actually the reports that he was martyred seem to be based on confusing him with another Hippolytus, actually a mythical Hippolytus, who was the son of Theseus and who was mythically killed by a bunch of mythical wild horses.

- As a final point, at the risk of sounding frivolous, "Hippoly-tus" just sounds like the name of a saint. With a name like that, living when he did and being a bishop and a theologian and writing lots of great religious treatises, including his famous Jew-hating tract, how could he not be a saint?

So take your pick of any one of these theories as to why Hippoly-tus is a saint or come up with one of your own. I think it was his Jew hating that put him over the top, but that's just me. Bottom line: Hip-polytus is the only anti-pope who is a saint, so he wins the award as the saintliest anti-pope.

OK. That was a rather lengthy explanation of an Anti-Pope Award, so let's make the rest of the awards real quick hitters:

Mistaken Identity Award: This goes to Anti-Pope Felix II. He was confused with another Felix, i.e., Pope St. Felix I, who was supposedly a martyr. As a result of this confusion Felix II's name was included in the Roman Martyrology as a saint with a feast day of July 29, but today nobody accepts him as a legitimate saint—because he's not. What's funny is that Felix I wasn't a martyr either. His feast day is May 30.

Three's a Crowd Award: This award is a tie. Two popes were op-posed by three different anti-popes. Boniface IX was opposed by Robert of Geneva (aka Clement VII), Pedro de Luna (aka Benedict XIII) and Baldassare Cossa (aka John XXIII); and Pope Gregory XII was opposed by Pedro de Luna (aka Benedict XIII), Baldasarre Cossa (aka John XXIII) and Pietro Philarghi (aka Alexander V).

Anti-Pope Cluster Fuck Award: Another tie! And I have to say that the anti-poping in both cases gets a bit ridiculous: Pope Paschal

II was opposed by not one, not two, not three, but four different anti-popes: Guibert (aka Clement III), Theodoric, Aleric and Maginulf (aka Sylvester IV). Pope Alexander III had four guys against him too: Octavius (aka Victor IV), Pascal III, Callistus III and Innocent III. Hey, I guess those were just wild and wooly times.

Life Is Short Award: This goes to Anti-Pope Dioscorus. Right before Pope Felix IV died in 530, he named his pal Boniface as the new pope. Obviously Felix liked Boniface, but apparently not many other people did. In fact, 60 out of 67 of the Roman priests who voted for popes back then rejected Boniface and named Dioscorus the new pope. So Dioscorus was the popular guy at the time. Unfortunately he died a couple of weeks later, and Boniface got all of the Roman priests to flip flop and change their support to him. So for Boniface it was all's well that ends well, but for Dioscorus not only was he dead but Boniface turned around and had him anathematized, which means he was formally excommunicated. I'm not sure how much Dioscorus cared about being anathematized since he was already dead and the anathema decree was reversed five years later by Pope Agapetus (Boniface was dead by then too), but the whole story just goes to show that success and fame are fleeting and life is really short. So I would like to give Dioscorus a very well-deserved Life Is Short Award.

What Would Jesus Say Award: This story reminds me of why I was so sorry when *The Sopranos* went off the air. When Pope John XIII died in 972, Benedict VI became pope, but John's brother Crescentius the Elder threw Benedict in jail and named Boniface VIII pope. Boniface promptly murdered Benedict. A month later there was pressure to oust Boniface as pope, and he had to flee to Constantinople—but not before he robbed the treasury of the Vatican Basilica. At this point Benedict VII was named pope. Nine years later, when the heat had finally died down and Benedict VII was dead, Boniface returned and threw Benedict's successor, John XIV, in jail, where he died four months later. All of this nastiness finally did catch up with Boniface. A little over a year later he was dead, probably as a result of having been murdered, although that is not clear. What is recorded is that, however he died, his corpse was dragged through the streets and deposited naked at the foot of the statue of Marcus Aurelius, which stood at the Lateran Palace. I think everybody would agree that Boniface deserves a reward for his relentless depravity. In recognition of said depravity, I bestow upon him the What Would Jesus Say Anti-Pope Award.

Best Nickname: This award goes to Robert of Geneva aka Anti-Pope Clement VII. After approving the massacre of 4,000 people in Cesena, Italy, to put down a rebellion, he was known affectionately as the Executioner of Cesena.

Last of the Mohicans Award: This award is given provisionally to Amadeus of Savoy aka Anti-Pope Felix V, who was anti-pope from 1439-1449, because he was in fact he last anti-pope to date. I say "to date" because—wishful thinking—I see no reason why there could not be another anti-pope in the future—maybe an anti-pope who calls for the ordination of women or an out-of-the-closet gay anti-pope who tells his in-the-closet gay fellow bishops to cut the anti-gay bigotry. Not very likely but we can always hope—and pray.

THE POPE'S GETUP

Who's the fanciest-dressing dude that walks the planet Earth? No doubt about it. That's the pope. He wins hands down. He may have had some competition at one point from Liberace, but his closet is closed. Elton John came close, too, with his Mozart costume and his animal suits, but Sir Reginald has calmed down a bit in recent years. In fact, there's only one person who has ever out-coutured the pope. That's Lady Gaga, and she had to wear meat to beat him.

It doesn't matter which pope we're talking about either. All the gear comes with the job—and it's a lot of gear.

It must take the pope longer to get ready for the day than the contestants on RuPaul's Drag Race. He just has so many things to put on. It's so much stuff I wonder if he cheats a little bit and just leaves half of it on when he goes to bed at night. That would give him a little bit of a head start on the next day.

Obviously the pope wasn't always this much of a fancy Dan. I'll bet St. Peter wore the same ragged tunic for forty years. Maybe he had a spare, but I doubt it. The vestment thing must have sort of grown and built up over the years until it took on a life of its own, and there just wasn't anybody around who had the nerve to put a stop to it—nobody who would stand up to the pope and say it's time to stop the madness. Here's the funny thing, though. Now that it's totally out of hand, it's also totally accepted. I never hear anybody question the fact that the pope walks around looking like the Christmas tree at Radio City. I guess it just seems normal by now. People look at this guy sporting a big pointy hat and wearing about eight layers of flashy clothes in the middle of August in Rome, and they think that's just the pope being the pope. That's what he wears. No big deal.

But when you go to make a list of the things the pope wears, you realize how weird his clothing fetish really is. I have a Ph.D. in English, and I've never heard of most of these clothing items before. I've never heard of the words. Let me list some of them. I'll bet almost nobody knows what the hell any of these things are:

- the pallium
- the zucchetto
- the mozzetta
- the cincture
- the subcinctorium
- the falda
- the morse
- the camauro
- the fanon

See. I wasn't kidding. I'll bet you could ask a thousand people and not one person would know what a single one of those items was. I left off the list things that are pretty weird that I think at least some people have heard of, like a mitre or a chasuble. I also left out things that are kind of weird but also self-explanatory like papal slippers and the papal tiara. I'm quite certain that Jesus never wore a tiara.

I was going to explain what all of these weird items of clothing are, but I'm not. Sorry. If you're interested, you should just look them up yourself. All I have to say is just think how revolutionary it would be if some day, the pope dropped all this vestment nonsense and just wore a sweater vest and a freshly ironed pair of slacks like Rick Santorum or even dressed down a little bit and wore a soccer jersey and a pair of low rise jeans. If he did, it would be a pretty good sign that things were finally changing.

CLEANSING MY PALATE

Way to Go!

It's no fun being negative all the time. Well, actually it is. It's great fun. Never underestimate the positive energy you can get from total negativity. Try it some time and you'll see. It's true. But having said that, I'd like to take a break and give some props to the church for the good things it does. Really? Yes, really. By "the church," I mean the people and programs that serve and support people in need all around the world. Here we go:

The Sisters of Social Service meet "the needs of the poor and neglected through direct service and contemporary social action for change." Their work includes providing centers for homeless teens and marginalized women, parenting education for inner-city mothers, foster care for infants in crisis, meals and companionship for the elderly and neighborhood centers for low-income families. That is all so beautiful. Find out more about the sisters by going to their website at www.sistersofsocialservice.com.

The Sisters of Bon Secours are dedicated to caring for the sick and dying. The sisters bring health care to people where they live, including providing clinics for migrant workers and utilizing mobile health care vans. They also provide care in hospitals, hospices, assisted living and nursing care facilities. They strive to further the cause of social justice and peace throughout the world and are part of UNANIMA International, a 16,000 member, global organization formed through a coalition of seven religious organizations that fights for human rights and social development. Find out more by going to the sisters' website at www.bonsecoursvocations.org. You will be inspired.

Peter Maurin and **Dorothy Day** founded the Catholic Worker Movement back in the 1930s. Their work lives on today through dozens of Catholic Worker houses across the country that serve the poor and stand up for social justice. For more information, including a directory of Catholic Worker facilities across the US, go to www.catholicworker.org.

The Ursuline Sisters are dedicated to teaching, feeding the hungry, aiding the homeless and responding to the needs of people with HIV/AIDS. They are a sponsor of the Dorothy Day House in Youngstown, Ohio, which provides meals every day to people who would otherwise go hungry. Check out the sisters at www.theursulines.org.

I've known about **Maryknoll** since I was a little kid through *Maryknoll Magazine*. Maryknoll is actually three organizations, the Maryknoll Fathers and Brothers (aka the Catholic Foreign Mission Society of America), the Maryknoll Sisters (aka the Maryknoll Sisters of St. Dominic) and the Maryknoll Lay Missioners (aka the Catholic Foreign Mission Society). There are affiliates who support the work of Maryknoll as well. These dedicated men and women are at work all over the world building communities that support peace, ecology, social and economic justice. Check out:

www.maryknoll.org

www.maryknollogc.org

http://www.maryknollsisters.org

www.maryknollsociety.org.

www.maryknolllaymissioners.org

www.maryknollmagazine.org.

The Quixote Center is a grassroots organization founded more than 35 years ago by the late Bill Callahan, a former Jesuit priest, which fights for social justice and equality. The Quixote Center has a number of major programs, including the Quest for Peace, which "seeks peace and friendship with the people of Nicaragua by advocating just US policies and supporting Nicaraguan human development organizations"; Haiti Reborn, which "builds grassroots support in the United States for improved policies toward the people of Haiti, and supports Haitian development organizations"; and Catholics Speak Out, which promotes "equality for all men and women in both church and society." The Quixote Center has a vision of equality in society that I wholeheartedly embrace. The Center "supports gender equality, including ordination for women; the civil rights of gay, lesbian, bisexual, and transgender persons; and advocates for an end to the rule of celibacy for Catholic clergy." Hey, I would pray every day for that vision to become a reality if there were indeed anybody to pray to (although I'd still be extremely annoyed that I would have to persuade the object of my prayers to help). For more information on the Quixote Center, which is based in College Park, MD, go to www.quixote.org.

Network: A National Catholic Social Justice Lobby was founded in 1971 by 47 nuns at a meeting at Trinity College in Washington, DC. The mission of the organization was "to shape a new ministry of justice." Over the past four decades Network has focused on a broad range of issues, including economic justice, immigration reform, healthcare, peacemaking, ecology and women's rights. In 2012 Network organized the "Nuns on the Bus" tour, which traveled through nine states to protest Congressman Paul Ryan's proposed cuts to social safety net programs. In 2013 the "Nuns on the Bus" took to the road again to promote immigration reform. You can learn more about Network and the "Nuns on the Bus" by going to www.networklobby.org.

Catholic Relief Services (CRS) provides emergency relief as well as long-term developmental services to people across the world. They work with local church agencies, faith-based partners, NGOs and governmental organizations to provide a broad range of services and programs, focusing on such issues as agro-economic development and environmental stewardship, education, hunger, health with a particular focus on HIV/AIDS, peace building, water and sanitation, human trafficking, providing microfinance support, providing social safety nets for people with little or no resources and of course emergency relief. For example, in response to the earthquake in Haiti, CRS built more than 10,000 shelters, provided more than 10 million meals to a million people, organized medical teams to perform more than a thousand emergency surgeries and hired more than 12,000 people in temporary cash-for-work programs. Find out more about the tremendous work that Catholic Relief Services does at www.crs.org.

Pax Christi is a global grassroots peace and justice movement that engages on a wide range of issues, including human rights, human security, disarmament and the role that religion plays in fomenting violence. In keeping with this mission, the US Pax Christi organization announced in 1999 a twenty-year initiative called "Brothers and Sisters

All" "to transform Pax Christi USA into an anti-racist, multicultural Catholic peace and justice movement," a goal that recognizes that we all need to dedicate ourselves every day to embracing diversity and tolerance. For Pax Christi International, go to www.paxchristi.net. For Pax Christi USA, check out www.paxchristiusa.org.

Catholic Charities is a nationwide network of Catholic agencies and affiliates that provides a host of programs, including adoption services, housing counseling, family strengthening, combating human trafficking, initiatives to fight poverty and promote racial equality, initiatives to improve the environment and fight global warming and emergency relief services. Catholic Charities also engages in advocacy with policy makers to pass legislation to reduce poverty. Learn more about Catholic Charities at www.catholiccharitiesusa.org.

The **Cristo Rey** network consists of more than two dozen Catholic high schools that provide innovative work-study programs to help inner-city young men and women with limited educational options prepare themselves for college. At a time when many Catholic high schools are closing, Cristo Rey is expanding with plans to start schools across the country. Check out www.cristoreynetwork.org for more information.

And while we're talking about education, I would like to recognize the great Catholic colleges and universities throughout the US that provide so many students with the opportunity to learn and grow and pursue their life goals—schools such as Villanova, St. Joseph's and LaSalle from my hometown, Philly; Boston College, Holy Cross, Providence, Fairfield, Fordham, St. John's, St. Bonaventure, St. Peter's, Scranton, Seton Hall, Catholic University, Georgetown, Xavier,

DePaul, the three Loyola's, Marquette, Creighton, Gonzaga, the University of San Francisco and, of course, in my opinion, the greatest Catholic University of them all—my alma mater, the University of Notre Dame. What an inspiring group of institutions led by so many brilliant and dedicated educators.

Way to go, everybody!

In talking here about the amazing work that the Catholic Church does, I've been focusing on programs and initiatives, but obviously it's all about the people. There are tens of thousands of dedicated sisters, brothers, priests and lay people, representing a diverse range of beliefs, who work tirelessly every day to minister to the poor and hungry and to advocate for peace and equality. These are truly the People of God. These people are the Church, and when I think of the courage and love and the selflessness of these people and the beautiful work they do, I have to tell you, it brings a tear to my eye. Personally, I would just like to say is thank you to each and every one of you from the bottom of my heart. I love you all.

GO TO THE DEVIL

Give the Devil His Due

I just can't seem to do it. Whenever I try to imagine what it's like to live inside the brain of somebody who believes in the devil, I last about one second and then go running for the cranial exits—screaming. It's just too scary. Not the image of the devil that the devil-believing brain conjures up—that's not scary at all. What's scary is the brain itself. How in the world after centuries of science and decades, at least, of free access to public education, does anybody still believe in the devil?

At least one of our esteemed candidates for the 2012 Republican presidential nomination, Rick Santorum, believes in the devil. Actually I would have been shocked if he had said he didn't believe in the devil—that just wouldn't fit with his far right conservative Catholic theocratic worldview. But his remarks about the devil in a 2008 speech at Ave Maria University, including the statement that "Satan has his sights on the United States of America," created a bit of a stir in the media. Santorum's campaign was annoyed at the negative attention. They said it was ridiculous because after all Rick's devil belief is totally in the mainstream of American thought—and, of course, they were right. Amazing. But most Americans do believe in the devil. Harris and Gallup polls put the percentage of devil believers at 62 percent and 70 percent, respectively. I don't quite know how to factor in mendacity when it comes to belief in the devil. Would more people lie and say they believe in the devil because they think most people do, or would more lie and say they don't believe out of embarrassment? But even if the real number is lower, like say 50 percent, it would still mean that around 100 million Americans believe in the devil. That makes me feel real creepy. It means that when I go out to places like the grocery store and the deli and the Department of Motor Vehicles that I'm rubbing elbows with a whole bunch of people who wake up each morning and go to bed each night believing that the devil really exists. He may be a spirit, but he's just as real as a slice of pepperoni pizza or crab grass or the nose on your fucking face.

What do we know about the devil? Nothing, of course, but what information is out there? Just what are the sources of devil information?

Well, I'm pretty sure that the very first description of the devil is the one in Genesis with Adam and Eve in the Garden of Eden, and in that account the devil is a talking serpent. Right. That alone I think is enough to make any intelligent person question the whole devil thing. The only other place I ever encountered a talking serpent was on the old cartoon "Beany and Cecil." Cecil the Sea Sick Sea Serpent talked—actually with a bit of a lisp. I enjoyed the cartoon, but I never believed that Cecil existed outside of the cartoon.

The devil also shows up in the Book of Job, and here it's a different story altogether. In Job he's not a talking serpent, he's a guy named Satan, and it's clear that he and his Hell's Angels entourage are all pals with God. They sort of hang out together in some kind of a celestial "Man Cave" and play a game of torturing Job. The devil says if he tortures Job, he'll curse God. God says no way, Job's the best guy in the world, so go ahead and torture him—you'll see. Satan kills Job's children, kills all his livestock, destroys everything he has and then gives him a really bad case of boils all over his body. To be honest—and this is pretty funny—I don't know that you can really say that God won the bet because while Job doesn't exactly say "Fuck you, God," he does question how God could be just and good and treat him this way. That is a very fair question. Where does all of the suffering and the evil originate, if not from God? In the end, God comes on like a big bully and tells Job to shut the fuck up and quit complaining, but then he gives him back more livestock than he lost and some new children, too—not Job's real children. They stay dead. Just a new set of children, which I guess means that God thinks that one set of children is as good as another. Just like livestock.

Another famous appearance of the devil is when he shows up in the desert after Jesus has been out there for forty days and forty nights fasting. In this case the devil comes across as a total moron. At one point he actually tells Jesus that he'll give him ownership of every-thing he sees on earth if he'll just get down and worship him. As I point out in my book, *You Got to Be Kidding*, this is like somebody pointing to my house and saying I'll let you live there if you kiss my ass. It's a good thing for the devil that he pulled this shit on Jesus, who must have been pretty weak at the time from fasting and who was the original "turn the cheek guy." He just told the devil to get lost. I would have beaten the shit out of him.

I would say that those are the three most famous appearances of the devil, and he's impressive only one out of three times. I'll give him his due. In the Book of Job, he fucks up Job pretty good, although he has to get permission from God to do it, which really means that God is the one fucking up Job, and the devil is just his hit man. The serpent in the garden thing is like a Grimm's fairy tale, and his would-be star turn in the desert with Jesus is a grotesque embarrassment.

The funny thing is really this: if there is a devil, doesn't that reflect pretty badly on an all-knowing, all-powerful God? We're supposed to believe that God created the devil, knowing that he would rebel and cause all sorts of trouble forever and ever. That's like believing that God really wanted to create Black Holes so that he could watch them suck up his beautiful creation like gigantic cosmic vacuum cleaners. The only way that it would make any sense for God to create the devil is so that he could blame all of the bad stuff he created on somebody else. You know, just shift the blame and say don't look at me, I'm all-good. Blame the devil. He's the bad guy.

Now that explanation actually makes a little sense. That I could maybe believe.

BE GONE, SATAN!

A lot of people don't just believe in the devil. They believe he can possess you, too. That means he can somehow get inside your body and fuck you up.

Now let's be clear. There's only one devil, so almost all possessions would not be by the devil himself but by one of his demon friends. Maybe every once in awhile the devil does possess somebody himself just to stay sharp and keep his hand in the possession game. But not usually. So it's sort of like a Santa Claus sighting. At Christmas time you see Santas all over the place, but do you ever see the real Santa? You'd probably have to go to the North Pole, and even then you might not see him.

But how does the devil or his demon friends actually get inside you and possess you? This isn't very clear. It appears though that since demons are spirits, they do not have to gain entry through bodily orifices—like shooting up your nose or flying up your asshole. Apparently if you engage in certain behaviors, you can become vulnerable to demonic possession—like when your immune system is compromised and bang! You get sick from a virus or a bacterial infection. Fr. Gabriele Amorth, an exorcist of the diocese of Rome and the founder of the International Association of Exorcists, claimed in 2010 that he had performed more than 70,000 exorcisms. I would think that qualifies him as a real expert on demonic possession, although the 70,000 number does strike me as falling into the same factoidal category as

Wilt Chamberlain's claim of having had sex 20,000 times. Or was it sex with 20,000 women? Yeah, that was it. Anyway, if Fr. Amorth started performing exorcisms in 1986, the year he became the exorcist of the diocese of Rome, that would work out to eight exorcisms a day, which is sort of like saying that the possessed went to Jiffy Lube to get cured. Be that as it may, I'll take the good father's word that he's done a lot of exorcisms, and so he may be able to explain how people become possessed. In fact, he says there are four ways that it can happen:

1. God lets the devil or his demon friends possess you (so here we are back again in the Book of Job).

2. You can be cursed. (Fr. Amorth says curses are real, and certain curses can give demons access.)

3. If you're really sinful, like engage in what Fr. Amorth calls "sexual perversions" or have an abortion that opens you up to possession.

4. If you expose yourself to evil—like get involved with the occult, view pornography or horror movies, listen to rock music, attend rock concerts or go to clubs. If you do any of these things, it's like you're putting out a welcome sign and inviting demons to come inside.

Another exorcist, Father José Antonio Fortea, of the diocese of Alcalá de Henares (Madrid), has a different list. He says you're liable to get possessed if you—

1. Make a pact with the devil (or demons)

2. Take part in spiritualist sessions, satanic cults or esoteric rites

3. Offer your child to Satan

4. Are a victim of witchcraft (i.e., a spell)

It's a little confusing that the lists are so different. Both lists do mention the occult, but Fr. Fortea doesn't say anything about God doing a Job number on you or the dangers of sexual perversion, abortion, pornography, horror movies, rock music, rock concerts or clubs, and Fr. Amorth fails to mention making a pact with the devil or offering him your child. Are the two lists right when combined, or are both lists partly right and partly wrong? Also, I would think that the devil would be happy if you gave him your child, although I'm not really sure what this means. Does your child go and live with him, and where would that be, or does your child stay with you, or is it sort of like joint custody with visitation? Somebody needs to explain all of this to me. However it works, why would the devil decide to possess you after you just gave him your child? I know he can't be trusted at all, but why would he bother hassling you at this point unless maybe you were really pushing him on the money part of the deal and he got pissed off.

Anyway, however it happens, there's no doubt that demonic possession is really nasty. We've all seen *The Exorcist*, which by the way is Fr. Amorth's favorite movie (I thought he said to stay away from horror movies). He claims that it's basically an accurate portrayal of demonic possession and exorcism. That would mean that symptoms of demonic possession might include the possessed person spider walking down stairs, puking green slime, masturbating with a crucifix, growling in a really weird devil voice, talking backwards and spinning their head around 360°. The crucifix is obviously a bad choice for a dildo since it can cut you up pretty good if you're a woman and it's probably not that stimulating if you're a man. Maybe a rubber cross would work, but I suggest just using your hand. The rest of the behaviors are of course a little strange, especially the head spinning, which requires either some very special neck muscles or maybe having your own special effects crew nearby. But however strange, exactly how would one know that all of this crazy shit is happening because the person is possessed? After all, maybe they're just looking for a little extra attention.

There are a number of other supposed symptoms of demonic possession, including having superhuman strength and getting really bent out of shape at anything holy or religious. But it really does seem that there is no definitive way of knowing if somebody is possessed as opposed to being crazy or a fraud. I'm sure if you ask Fr. Amorth or Fr. Fortea, they would echo the famous Potter Stewart line about obscenity and say they know demonic possession when they see it, and when they do, they're ready to slide down the fire pole and go to the rescue of the poor possessed individual. In fact, as I pointed out, that's exactly what Fr. Amorth says he did eight times a day for almost a quarter century.

Now once these exorcist guys slide down the fire pole and set out to exorcize a demon, what the heck do they do? Well, to me this is the really disappointing part of the whole demonic possession thing. The exorcists don't go in with a proton pack and zap the demon like a ghostbuster would or whip out some really esoteric chants and incantations that would scare the shit out of even the most demonic demon from the lowest depths of hell. No. They just recite a list of saints' names, say some prayers and tell the demon to leave. Imagine if a bouncer tried that on some drunk asshole in a local club. Sorry, but it just wouldn't work, not even on your typical garden-variety noisy drunk. So how would it work on a demon from hell or on the devil himself? So as hard as it is for me to believe that any of these crazy fucking people are really possessed, it's even harder for me to believe that, if they were possessed, the demons would leave because a priest said a few prayers and told them to be gone in the name of God. Aren't demons sort of like convicted murderers who have been sentenced to life in prison without parole in states without the death penalty? I mean they're already demons; they're already condemned to spend eternity in hell or else roaming around the universe looking for people to possess, so what can really happen to them? God has already thrown the book at them. Why should they give a fuck about a couple of prayers and a priest telling them to beat it?

Now—full disclosure—I have never attended an exorcism, nor have I ever interviewed any demons to get their point of view on the efficacy of the Church's Ritual of Exorcism. I would therefore like to offer an open invitation to any exorcist out there. Invite me to your next exorcism. I promise to cancel whatever plans I have and show up promptly to witness the demonic festivities. Fr. Amorth, Fr. Fortea⊠ that includes you. You know my name, so look up the number, as the Beatles once said.

As for all you demons out there, if any of you feel misunderstood and would like to tell your side of the story, look me up. I'm all ears.

SEX AND THE ETERNAL CITY

THE PURPOSE OF SEX

According to the Catholic Church, the purpose of sex is procreation. Of course, it's not just the Catholic Church that says this. Every Christian denomination says the same thing, and a whole lot of people believe it too.

I guess it is true that the bigger the lie, the more people believe it, and this is one of the biggest lies of all. I mean is there a single person in the entire history of the human race who experiences that first moment of sexual awareness and thinks, "Wow! There it is. It just kicked in. I am now feeling the urge to procreate. Thank you, puberty! I am now ready, willing and able to fulfill my obligation to perpetuate the species."

That has obviously never happened, but that apparently doesn't matter to the Catholic Church, all of the other Christian denominations and all of the people who believe that without question the purpose of sex is procreation. According to them, God planned it that way. He made sex feel good so that we'd want to procreate and ensure the survival of our species. If procreation were dull and boring, or if it were painful, like passing a kidney stone or getting your wisdom teeth out, the human race would have died out long ago. But God made sure in his infinite wisdom that our dicks get hard and our clits get stiff, and when boy meets girl, it just feels so damn good . . . and so, thanks be to God, we've been happily copulating and populating ever since.

Now you might think that there is actually something positive about this whole unlikely explanation of why sex feels so darn good. You might think that it means God approves of sex. After all, he's the one who decided to make it feel so good. I'm sorry to say, however, that you would be wrong, dead wrong.

If there's one thing the church is really good at, it's building maximum-security prisons of the mind. All it needs is a single idea that can serve as the corner stone and that's it. Case closed. That jailhouse is built. Supermax and built to last and guess what? You're inside.

Here's how the thinking goes: The purpose of sex is procreation. That is God's plan. Therefore, sex is only allowed within marriage and only when it allows for procreation. That means that the only permissible sexual act is intercourse between a man and a woman who are married to each other. This creates a rather striking duality. Coital sex with your spouse is sacred even if you can't stand the sight of each other and aren't even on speaking terms. But if you're having sex with somebody you're not married to, that is morally wrong, and if you're not only fucking, you're getting in a little oral sex as well maybe or some other fetishy thing that really gets your rocks off, but isn't going to make a baby, that is all contrary to natural law and morally wrong. So coital sex within marriage—that's all good, but sex outside of marriage or any sexual act other than intercourse—that's downright dirty. It's a mortal sin. It violates the natural order of creation. It violates your relationship with the Creator of the Universe, and if you keep on fucking around and never repent and don't change your sinful sexual ways, then, when you die, you're going straight to hell.

How's that for putting a damper on the party? Imagine. You're a twelve- year-old boy and you've just arrived in Puberty Junction. You just started growing pubes last week, and you get a raging hard on from almost anything. Maybe the school bus ran over a big pothole or maybe you happened to catch a glimpse of that sexy picture of Betty

Crocker on the box of a fudge brownie mix—whatever. Your dick is so hard you could rent it out as a jackhammer, and it's starting to move around in your pants like a cobra dancing to the sound of a street charmer's pungi. You've also just gotten the word from Father Bob and Sister Mary Timothy at Mother of Sorrows parochial school that if you even think for one nanosecond that you like the feeling that you get from your hard on and you take a second glance at Betty Crocker or hope that the bus driver runs over another pothole, you, my friend, have willingly given in to what Thomas Aquinas called "venereal plea-sure." And, you guessed it; you've just wracked up a big fat mortal sin. You haven't even touched yourself yet in an impure manner and you're already damned, so you might as well run to the nearest bathroom and bust your nut because you're already going to hell anyway.

Of course, fucking up the minds of impressionable twelve-year-olds over spontaneous hard-ons and impure thoughts doesn't even tell half the story of all the damage that the church's teaching on sex does. Suppose you're a twelve-year-old girl and you suddenly find yourself strangely attracted to that picture of Betty Crocker. Or maybe you're a twelve-year-old boy, and one day it suddenly occurs to you—you know, in a few of those artist renderings of Jesus, he actually looks kind of cute. And with that thought, you're dick lifts up its head and smiles.

Little lesbian girl and little gay boy, I'm sorry to have to tell you this, but homosexuality is a disorder. It's unnatural—at least accord-ing to the Catholic Church. It's always been that way and always will be. If you have any doubt, read the Bible. I would go directly to St. Paul. He'll tell you everything you need to know about how fucked up and perverted you are.

Now suppose you say, but I think I was born this way? It doesn't matter. God gives us all crosses to bear, and this one's yours. There's no use even asking why. Just think of the fact that you are homosexual as a wonderful opportunity to practice self-denial because that's exactly what you'll have to do if you want to be saved. There's no marriage for you because marriage is between a man and a woman. There's also no sex outside of marriage, so no sex for you either. The good news is that although the church views you as a disordered pervert, being a disordered pervert isn't in and of itself a sin. Furthermore, the church doesn't hate you. It just hates your sin, i.e., ever wanting to have sex or having sex. So long as you never have sex and in fact never even think of having sex, you're still eligible for heaven. Feel better now?

Of course, there's one more very important piece to the church's teaching on sex, and we must be sure not to forget it—and that is contraception. Even if you're heterosexual and you only have sex with your spouse, you're still not in the clear. Since the purpose of sex is procreation, you have to make sure that every single time you have sex you can make a baby. No birth control pill, no condom, no diaphragm, no IUD, no pulling out just in the nick of time—no, you need to go at it the old fashioned way flying blind on a wing and a prayer.

Start with a lie. End with a lie or maybe call it total denial. Even though contraception has crazily become controversial again with the Catholic Church objecting to providing contraceptives to its female employees and the Republican Party's attack on women, the fact is that almost nobody in the Catholic Church follows the church's teaching on contraception. If you have any doubt about that, just think of all your Catholic friends who are married and count the number of children they have.

In the Closet

When I was growing up, I didn't know the church was the closet.
I didn't know that was where you went if you were a closeted gay guy
and you really didn't want anybody to know, ever, that you were gay.
I didn't know that that was where you went if you not only wanted to
hide that you were gay from everybody else, but you wanted to hide it
from yourself, too. Now clearly some people did know this. Here's my
question: how did they find out? There was no email back then, so forget that. If there was a direct mail list, I wasn't on it. I mean nothing
ever came to the house, unless my parents saw the letter and ripped
it up. None of my friends ever mentioned getting a letter or a memo
from the Catholic Church saying, if you're gay and you don't want
anybody to know and you want everybody to think you're really good
and holy, become a priest.

I don't know. Maybe my friends and I didn't qualify as part of the
targeted demographic. Maybe there was a direct mail campaign led by
the Holy Spirit that identified closeted or potentially closeted gay kids
and let them all know that the church was looking for them. Otherwise how did so many of them end up there?

I have to tell you. I never wanted to be a priest, not for one second. I remember a priest coming to our classroom back in maybe the
fourth grade. The nun, wanting to impress the priest, asked how many
of the boys in the class wanted to be a priest, and almost every one
of those fucking conforming assholes raised their hand. The only boys

who didn't were me and a kid named Robert Dunn. The nun asked Robert, what do you want to be when you grow up? She was apparently incredulous that every single boy wasn't ready to join the priest army. Robert replied somewhat incongruously that he wanted to be a bachelor, which of course didn't preclude becoming a priest, so Robert was just a little bit out of it, I guess. Then the nun asked me what I wanted to be, and I said, a baseball player. That to me back then was cool. Being a priest was not cool at all. It was like saying you wanted to spend your life in church, which was like committing a crime in front of a cop and saying, take me to jail.

I think out of all of those boys in my class only one actually became a priest—he's a Jesuit priest. He teaches at a Catholic university, and I'm pretty darn sure he's gay. He was a friend of mine. Other kids made fun of him because they thought he was a sissy—that was the word back then. He and I used to walk home from school together pretty frequently discussing politics when we were about twelve. He was a Republican, and I was a Democrat. I really enjoyed those discussions. My father noticed because a lot of times we would get to my house and were really into the discussion and would just keep on talking. My friend spoke in what might be called, especially back then, an effeminate voice and had a lot of effeminate gestures. One day when I came into the house after talking to my friend, my father said, "Why are you talking to him?"

I said, "What do you mean?"

My father said, "Isn't he a sissy?" making a kind of disgusted and dismissive grimace.

I think I said something like, "We like to talk." I always hated that comment from my father.

Anyway my friend never told me that he got the letter in the mail, but maybe he did. I don't know how much in or out of the closet he is now, but he did join the priest club, and, as I said, he's still a priest.

I could speculate further on why there are so many gay priests when the church is anti-gay. But it's just so weird, it may be better not to speculate about it—even if the speculations landed pretty close to the truth. Instead of speculating. I would really like to find out. It would be worth a book all by itself.

So I'm inviting all of you guys who are gay, closeted or not, and who seriously thought about becoming priests or who went into the seminary and dropped out or who went all the way and became priests—whether or not you're still priests—to please contact me. I'd love to know your story—whatever it is.

The Catholic Church is all about mysteries—it really loves the whole "it's a mystery" thing. Well, as far as I'm concerned, this is the biggest mystery of all. Gay men—why did you join or want to join an organization that says your sexual orientation is a perversion? Why did you join or want to join an organization that says that homosexual sex is a sin? Why did you or do you represent that bigoted point of view against yourself, the entire LGBT community and all people who stand up for freedom and equality? Why?

Contact me. I'd love to get to the bottom of this mystery.

WOMEN'S REPRODUCTIVE RIGHTS

What are women's reproductive rights, according to the Catholic Church? That's easy. They don't have any.

The Catholic Church's message to women is this: Your bodies are intended by God to produce babies. Your true identity is fulfilled in motherhood. That is your ultimate purpose in God's plan.

Basically if you're a woman, you have two choices regarding sexuality and reproduction. You can remain single and a virgin or you can marry a man and become a receptacle for your husband's sperm. In effect, you become a baby-making machine.

The church does not allow sex outside of heterosexual marriage. To have sex, you have to marry a person of the opposite sex. If you're gay, there's no sex for you and no marriage for you. If you're a woman and you marry a man, you are not supposed to deny your husband sex and when you have sex with him, whatever you do while having sex, if he ejaculates, he must deposit his sperm in your vagina. If he deposits his precious sperm anywhere else, you have both committed a mortal sin. That means you must expose yourself to his sperm every time he ejaculates without protection against disease or pregnancy. It's a pretty clear choice: risk disease and pregnancy or risk going to hell.

Either/or. Virgin or sperm receptacle. That stark dichotomy epitomizes the church's contemptuous view of women, a view that is profoundly denigrating and disrespectful. Women are not only subordinate to men; their very identity is subordinated to the act of conception and the role of motherhood.

What is more personal than the decision of whether or not you want to expose yourself to another person's DNA—in this case sperm—and whether or not you want to conceive a child? The answer is nothing. But the Catholic Church says that a woman in a heterosexual marriage has no choice.

It's hard to know how many people cheat on their spouses because you have to think that people who cheat might lie about their cheating. People lie about sex all of the time anyway. But clearly a lot of people do cheat. Is it 25 percent, 50 percent, higher? Whatever the number, there are many women who know or strongly suspect that their husband is cheating. What do they do when he comes to them for sex? Let's remember, there's also no divorce in the Catholic Church. If you are a Catholic woman and you are committed to following the church's teaching on contraception and reproduction and you are in a bad marriage—loveless, a cheating husband, a husband with an STD, an abusive husband—you are trapped.

What about abortion? Most people know that the Catholic Church is totally opposed to abortion. But what does that mean? Well, it means in part that the church opposes abortion even if a woman is raped. Right. If you're raped, the Catholic Church says you need to have the rapist's baby. The rapist could be a total stranger, as in a criminal or a psychopath or some random predator, or he could be your employer or a colleague or a friend or your father or your uncle or your brother. It could be anybody. It really doesn't matter whatever male found a way to get his sperm inside your vagina and connect with one of your eggs, you need to have his kid. That's the moral thing to do, that's the right thing to do because that fertilized egg implanted in you by a rapist has an immortal soul and it has a right to live on this planet even if it totally fucks up your entire life. So says the Catholic Church.

I think just about everybody understands that part of the Catholic Church's position on abortion. It's so disrespectful and so denigrating to women. There really are no words to describe the profound immorality of the church's moral teaching on women's reproductive rights.

But here's the thing. The church's teaching is even worse than insisting that you have to have a rapist's baby, and this is something that a lot of people, even Catholic women, may not know.

Being forced to have a rapist's baby is really horrific. Unspeakable. But at least you're still alive. Maybe something good will eventually happen in your life. Maybe after the rapist's kid is grown and moves out—who knows? Where there's life, there's hope, right? But if you're dead, it's all over. Well, here's the worst thing of all. The Catholic Church says that a woman cannot have an abortion even if her life is threatened. A lot of people, including Catholics, do not understand precisely what this means.

Let's take the case of an ectopic pregnancy as an example. In an ectopic pregnancy the fertilized egg is implanted outside the uterus, typically in a Fallopian tube. The condition is life threatening to the mother, and there is no hope that the fetus can survive. So the mother's life is in danger, and the fetus is doomed. Obviously you immediately abort the pregnancy using the medical procedure that is safest and least invasive to the mother. If the ectopic pregnancy is detected right away, the pregnancy may be terminated without surgery by injecting a drug called methotrexate at the location where there are cells developing. The Catholic Church opposes this procedure because its intent—hello—is to kill the developing fetus. Even though the fetus has no chance to survive and will threaten the mother's life in the absence of treatment, the church says this is murder. If a surgical procedure is performed at a later stage in the ectopic pregnancy, when perhaps the woman has already suffered damage to her Fallopian tube, then the church approves this procedure. The crazy logic is that the intent was to remove the tube, not the fetus that is in the tube, and therefore the death of the fetus is a secondary result of the medical procedure. I honestly do not know what the church's position is on performing a laparoscopy that is minimally invasive to terminate the pregnancy. The intent of this procedure, and of course the intent of the removal of the tube, is clearly to terminate the pregnancy and provide the woman with the proper medical treatment.

What can you say about the church's position on abortion? It is clear that the church goes beyond the position that a fertilized egg is a human being, that it has an immortal soul and that therefore its life is equal in importance to the life of the mother. In taking the position that a pregnancy cannot be terminated—intentionally, directly, noninvasively—to save the life of the mother, the church is undeniably stating that the life of the fertilized egg or fetus is more important than the life of the woman in whose body it is growing.

Is this woman hatred or what? Here's what I'd like to know. How come all of the female fertilized eggs and fetuses suddenly go down in value the moment they're born?

Also, it's absolutely clear to me that almost nobody, even the overwhelming majority of the most radical, so-called pro-life people would actually value a fertilized egg or a fetus more than they do a child. Just give anybody "Sophie's Choice" and see what they decide. In the book/movie *Sophie's Choice*, Sophie is on a train headed to Auschwitz when a Nazi doctor forces her to choose which of her two children will be immediately killed and which one will be allowed to accompany her to the concentration camp. She chooses her daughter over her son, is forever haunted by the choice, and eventually commits suicide.

If the choice were between a child and a fertilized egg, would anybody choose the egg? If the choice were between a child and a fetus, would anybody choose the fetus? If somebody did, what would that say about them? It would say that they are fucking nuts. That's what it would say, and yet clearly the Catholic Church does value a fertilized egg more than the fertilized egg's mother. So what is going on here? I think it gets down to the subordination of women to the role of motherhood; it gets down to the exaggerated idea of self-sacrifice and self-denial that the Catholic Church teaches; it gets down to the idea that suffering is redemptive and the sick fixation on martyrdom and living for the next life rather than this one. But if you clear away all of these considerations and complexities, there remains at the root of the church's profoundly immoral position on women's reproductive rights, a single, undeniable, ugly reality—total disrespect for and denigration of "Woman" herself. Clearly, without that fundamental disrespect, none of the other positions or views would follow.

If you don't agree, does the phrase "Adam's Rib" ring a bell?

CONTRACEPTION AND DEVELOPING COUNTRIES

It's a no-brainer to educate people to protect themselves against sexually transmitted diseases, especially HIV/AIDS—right? It's a no-brainer to educate people only to have children if they have the means and the commitment to take care of them. It's a no-brainer that in parts of the world where people are suffering from extreme poverty, overpopulation and starvation, and where HIV/AIDS has reached epidemic proportions, all members of the international community— governments, health care organizations, educational institutions and religious institutions—need to work together to limit the spread of STDs and to slow population growth.

Yes, it is a no-brainer. But not for the Catholic Church. The Catholic Church opposes contraception, including the use of condoms everywhere and at all times even though proper and consistent use of condoms would dramatically reduce the spread of HIV/AIDS, and would help limit population growth. According to the Catholic Church, contraception is intrinsically evil. In fact, the most extreme Catholic view is that contraception is responsible for sexual promiscuity and the spread of sexually transmitted disease because it promotes sex without the consequence of conception. More sex equals more disease—never mind that condoms prevent disease—and frankly, if you get sick from having sex it serves you right. In fact, condoms are actually bad because they prevent the spread of disease and therefore reduce even further the consequences of having sex.

In recent years the most powerful proponents of the Catholic Church's deadly position on condom use and contraception, particularly in reference to developing countries, have been Blessed Mother Teresa, Blessed Pope John Pail II and Pope Benedict XVI. Mother Teresa and Pope John Paul II were exceptionally militant on the subject of contraception, insisting that there were no exceptions to the church's ban. The argument that the use of condoms can significantly reduce the spread of disease and minimize suffering was effectively beside the point as far as Mother Teresa was concerned. You were wasting your breath if you talked compassion with that lady. She was a big time believer in how suffering is redemptive and brings you closer to Jesus who suffered and died on the cross. Indeed, the phoniness of her reputation as a selfless humanitarian is exposed by the fact that her facilities for the homeless, the sick and the dying provided primitive medical care and minimal pain relief even for patients in the end stages of terminal disease.

Pope John Paul II spoke out tirelessly against contraception. It was one of his main themes as pope. Here are just a few quotes:

Addressing a group of priests in 1983, the pope said that "contraception is to be judged objectively so profoundly unlawful as never to be, for any reason, justified. To think or to say the contrary is equal to maintaining that, in human life, situations may arise in which it is lawful not to recognize God as God." So if you use birth control pills, or if you wear a condom while you're having sex, it's the same as maintaining that God is not God. Say what?

In 1990 in a homily delivered in Mwanza, Tanzania, the pope used the term "unspeakable crime" to describe abortion and asserted that the use of contraception threatened "the sanctity of Marriage."

Indeed, he referred to "methods of birth control that are contrary to the 'truth' of married love as a 'gift' by which husband and wife become cooperators with God in giving life to a new human person." On the subject of "unspeakable crime," as of 2011, an estimated 35 million people have died of AIDS, and approximately 34 million people were living with the disease. In 2012 almost 870 million people suffered from chronic malnutrition.

In 1997 the Vatican's Pontifical Council for the Family issued a *Vade Mecum* (i.e., a handbook) *for Confessors Concerning Some Aspects of the Morality of Conjugal Life*. The document includes this statement: "The Church has always taught the intrinsic evil of contraception, that is, of every marital act intentionally rendered unfruitful. This teaching is to be held as definitive and irreformable. Contraception is gravely opposed to marital chastity." "Marital chastity"—Wow! According to the Catholic Church you can only have sex when you're married, and then when you're married, you have to practice "marital chastity." Of course, as many married people discover, "marital chastity," aka "no sex," is the typical, unhappy outcome of marriage.

In 2005 after the Catholic Agency for Overseas Development issued a paper calling for a range of approaches to fight AIDS, while acknowledging the reality that in many impoverished countries people are forced to become sex workers in order to support themselves, and after a public discussion among church officials on the subject of contraception, Pope John Paul II issued the following statement: "The Holy See . . . considers that it is necessary above all to combat [HIV/AIDS] in a responsible way by increasing prevention, notably through education about respect of the sacred value of life and formation of the correct practice of sexuality, which presupposes chastity and fidelity." OK. Maybe when Catholic priests start practicing chastity, we'll take a little more seriously the pope's insistence that all of us who haven't taken a vow of celibacy should stop fucking or just fuck our spouses.

Pope Benedict XVI has continued to champion the church's hard-line position on contraception with one possible exception. Recently he said that it may be a lesser evil for persons with an STD who are intent on having sex to use a condom so that they do not infect their partners. You think? Any sane person would agree that it is better to take precautions not to infect another person than to expose them to disease. The pope's "sky is blue" type statement on the efficacy of condoms to prevent the transmission of disease has been viewed as a softening of the church's position on contraception. That rather charitable interpretation of the pope's statement ironically shows how out of touch the church really is. How about viewing it as a "lesser evil" for people intent on committing the incredibly evil act of having sex to use condoms to protect themselves and their partners from disease? Oh, no! The church will never say that. That would mean sex without consequences, and that might encourage people to, God forbid, have more sex.

After more than three decades of education, new HIV infections and deaths from AIDS have dropped to the their lowest levels since the disease peaked in the late 1990s. As a result of intensive research and the development of new treatment therapies, HIV is becoming a manageable chronic disease rather than a death sentence for people who have access to these new treatment therapies.

No thanks to Blessed Mother Teresa, Blessed Pope John Paul II, Pope Benedict XVI or the Catholic Church.

Sexual Abuse

There is no way to compare anything contemporary to the horrors of the Crusades and the Inquisition. The Crusades encompassed more than 275 years of genocidal slaughter against people because of their religious beliefs. The Inquisition was a systematic campaign of terror, torture and murder carried on for approximately 600 years, once again against people because of their religious beliefs. The Crusades and the Inquisition belong on any list of the greatest atrocities in human history. Having said that, I must state unequivocally that the sexual abuse of children and adolescents by Catholic priests, which we know went on for decades and may have gone on for centuries, and which was systematically covered up and in essence condoned by the leadership of the Catholic Church, represents a depth of evil that is unspeakable and immeasurable.

The abuse was so widespread that virtually everyone who grew up in the Catholic Church over the second half of the twentieth century would have known or had some acquaintance with a predatory priest. The abusers may have been their parish priest or pastor, a high school or college teacher, or perhaps a trusted counselor. Of course, everybody necessarily knows by name the leaders of the church who ignored the abuse, covered up the abuse, obstructed the investigation of the abuse and/or with full knowledge of the abuse deliberately reassigned abusers to new parishes or positions where they could continue to assault and rape innocent children and adolescents with impunity.

These leaders include high school principals, church administrators, pastors, bishops and cardinals. Many people know victims. Many people are victims. Some have come forward. Others have not. We do not know how many.

Blessed Pope John Paul II—the man some people think was one of the greatest men of the twentieth century and who is on the fast track to canonization—is one hundred percent responsible for the church's cover up and obstruction of the sex abuse investigation. He is also one hundred percent responsible for allowing the practice of the reassignment of sexual predators to go on. He could have ordered that there be an open and aggressive investigation. He could have ordered that all evidence of sexual abuse be immediately referred to the police. He did not. In fact, he did the opposite.

The pope ignored a 1984 memo from canon lawyer Fr. Thomas Doyle informing him that priests were sexually abusing children as well as a detailed report on the abuse that Doyle sent to every American bishop the following year. In fact, he ignored all of the countless reports of abuse throughout the years of his papacy. He even refused Cardinal Joseph Ratzinger's pleas that there be an investigation into allegations of sexual abuse against Cardinal Hans Hermann Groër, the Archbishop of Vienna. Indeed, despite the fact that Cardinal Bernard Law was forced to resign as archbishop of Boston as a result of the *Boston Globe's* investigation into sexual abuse by Boston priests, the pope subsequently rewarded him by naming him archpriest of the Papal Basilica of Santa Maria Maggiore in Rome. He was also appointed to the board of the Congregation of Bishops, which selects new bishops. John Paul also continued to support his friend Fr. Marcial Maciel Degollado, the founder of the Legionaries of Christ religious order and a huge fundraiser, despite numerous accusations that he was a sexual predator. In 1976 Bishop John R. McGann sent the pope a letter from Fr. Juan Vaca, a former Legion priest, with allegations of Maciel's abuse of him and twenty young Legionaries seminarians. They wrote to the pope again in 1978. When Vaca left the priesthood in 1989, he again wrote to the pope concerning Maciel's abuse. There was never any response from the pope. In nine men came forward with charges that Maciel had abused them while they studied under him in the 1940s and '50s. In addition to his having clearly been an abuser for many years, Maciel fathered six children with two different women. One of the women has claimed that Maciel abused her as a child. In 2005, just before John Paul died, Maciel resigned as head of the order. However, the Vatican did not formally denounce him until 2010, two years after he had died.

Pope John Paul II's refusal to vigorously investigate the countless allegations of priests sexually abusing minors is an absolute disgrace. There is no way to rationalize his responsibility or minimize his guilt. His shameful defense of predatory priests personifies the shame of the entire church.

As I mentioned, given how widespread the abuse was throughout the church, virtually everyone who grew up in the church in the latter half of the twentieth century would almost necessarily have known abusers. I knew several priests who were abusers. Monsignor Leonard Furmanski was my freshman religion teacher at Cardinal O'Hara High School in Springfield, PA. He was also the guidance counselor. I remember meeting with Fr. Furmanski about my college plans. I told him that I wanted to go to Notre Dame. After reviewing my academic record, he smiled, looked up at me and said he thought that I would be accepted. He was right. I did get accepted. I was the first person in my family to go to college, and I attended Notre Dame. As the oldest of eleven children in a working-class Irish Catholic family, I achieved what to them had seemed the Impossible Dream.

I had no idea that the priestly guidance counselor smiling at me from across the desk was a vicious predator who had victimized countless children and adolescents. The Philadelphia Grand Jury Report states flatly that Monsignor Furmanski, "sexually abused children throughout his 44 years as a teacher, principal, and pastor in the Archdiocese of Philadelphia." The report documents some of the rapes and sexual assaults perpetrated by Furmanski: For example, "as pastor during the 1980s at Sacred Heart parish in Swedesburg, [PA], Msgr. Furmanski started a sex education class for grade schoolers. He lay on top of a 12-year-old girl and rubbed his erect penis against her under the pretense of 'instructing' her in sex education. He also arranged sexual encounters between the girl and an altar boy." Note: His abuse of this girl went on for two years, three or four times a month. "Monsignor Furmanski later admitted to 'fondling' boys in the 1980s. He was accused by one altar boy of forcing him to perform oral sex."

In the Philadelphia Archdiocese, Secretary of the Clergy Monsignor William J. Lynn and Cardinal Anthony Joseph Bevilacqua were two of the most heinous offenders in protecting priests that they absolutely knew were raping children and adolescents, either leaving them in their current positions or reassigning them to other parishes or schools, where they would continue victimizing minors. Bevilacqua's predecessor, Cardinal John J. Krol, also protected and reassigned priests that he knew were child rapists. Here's what Lynn and Bevilacqua did in the case of Furmanski:

"Cardinal Bevilacqua left Msgr. Furmanski in ministry following an allegation in 1999 that the priest had instructed an 11-year-old altar boy to, as the boy described it, massage Monsignor's 'leg.' Despite evidence suggesting that sexual abuse had occurred, Secretary for Clergy William J. Lynn wrote to the cardinal that 'there is no reason for Furmanski not to return to the parish.'

"In 2002, Cardinal Bevilacqua left Msgr. Furmanski in ministry after learning that, as a teacher at Cardinal O'Hara High School in 1964, Msgr. Furmanski had sexually abused a freshman student after the boy confided to him about being raped by his algebra teacher in a janitor's closet at the school. The victim told Msgr. Lynn that Msgr. Furmanski abused him for months, fondling the boy naked and having him do the same in return." In fact, Furmanski was allowed to retire as a priest in 2004. He died in 2009.

Fr. Michael McCarthy was my sophomore biology teacher at Cardinal O'Hara. Despite the fact that a mother had complained that Fr. McCarthy had touched her son improperly at Cardinal O'Hara, Cardinal Bevilacqua appointed McCarthy to the position of administrator at St. Kevin's parish in Springfield, PA. The mother's complaint was originally ignored by Cardinal O'Hara principal Fr. Philip J. Cribben. Fr. Cribben had been my freshman English teacher. It was also discovered that Fr. McCarthy repeatedly took boys to his New Jersey beach house, got them drunk, slept nude with them and then masturbated them and himself. Knowing all of this, Cardinal Bevilacqua named McCarthy pastor of Epiphany of Our Lord Church in Norristown, PA. After numerous reports of McCarthy's sexual abuse of boys he was placed on unsupervised leave from 1993 until his retirement in 2003.

There were two other predator priests at Cardinal O'Hara when I was a student there that I knew of but who were not my teachers or counselors: Fr. John A. Cannon, a math teacher, and Fr. Raymond O. Leneweaver. Fr. Cannon sexually abused teenage boys at a summer camp from 1959 to 1964. He was accused of abuse by eight of the boys in 1964. The accusations were ignored except for the fact that he was transferred to another assignment. Who knows how many minors Cannon sexually abused throughout his career as a priest? Like so many other abusers he was allowed to continue as a priest in good standing, receiving one assignment after another, until his retirement in 2004. Leneweaver's story is absolutely unbelievable. From the early 1960s until 1980 there were countless accusations of Leneweaver raping and sexually abusing children. He himself began admitting to the rapes and abuse in the late '6os, but no action was ever taken against him except for transferring him to another position. According to Philadelphia Schools Chancellor Msgr. Francis J. Statkus, by 1980, when Leneweaver voluntarily withdrew from the priesthood, his sexual abuse was "so widespread that there were only two areas of the diocese where he could still be assigned." For the next twenty-five years Leneweaver continued to teach in public schools and to pose a dire threat to all of the children that he had contact with. Cardinal Bevilacqua, Msgr. Lynn and other church officials knew this and did nothing.

I knew one other sexual abuser. That would be Fr. James T. Burtchaell. He was my freshman theology teacher at Notre Dame. He was also chairman of the Theology Department and Provost of the University. Complaints that Burtchaell sexually abused students that he was counseling dated back to the 1970s, but he was not forced to resign his tenured position with the university until 1991.

I tell these stories of the predator priests that I knew or knew of along with the cover up of the atrocities that they committed because they are microcosms of what went on throughout the entire Catholic Church for at least decades, although I suspect we're talking centuries. The depth of evil represented by the depraved behavior of these priests and the attendant cover up is almost impossible to grasp. How could all of this be true? What is the explanation for such epic, ubiquitous, institutional abuse of defenseless children by the very people who you would think are most dedicated to protecting them—people who are supposed to be God's representatives on earth?

The next-to-last chapter of this book is a series of more than one hundred unanswered questions. Most of them are pretty funny. When it comes to the issue of the Catholic Church sex abuse scandal—and let's be absolutely clear and explicit here—that means thousands of Catholic priests raping and abusing children and adolescents for decade after decade and the entire hierarchy of the church, including the pope, covering it up and protecting the rapists—I have nothing but unanswered questions, and none of them are funny.

My first unanswered question is this: How is it that there were/are so many priests who were/are sexual abusers, child rapists, pedophiles, hebephiles, ephebophiles (just so I've covered all of these fucking predators)? I'm not usually into conspiracy theories, but maybe there is somehow some grand organizer or career adviser for child rapists on this planet, and he (it would have to be a he) sent out a memo to his special mailing list of child rapists telling them that the number one thing to be was a Catholic priest—you have unlimited access to children, unquestioned credibility and total support and protection from the entire hierarchy of the church. I didn't get this memo. Of course, I'm not a predator, so I'm not on the list. If anybody did get this memo, I'd like to see it, and I'd like to talk to you.

If there is no such memo, then how did so many predators know that the answer to all of their pedophiliac prayers was to become a priest? I would really like every single predatory, pedophiliac, hebephiliac, ephebophiliac priest to contact me and tell me your story. Was it just word of mouth? Is there a child rapist grapevine? What's going on here? Nobody has ever explained this. Don't tell me that priests became predators because they couldn't handle being celibate. That's nonsense. If you can't handle celibacy, you just go out and fuck an adult. You don't rape a child. Nobody becomes a child rapist later in life. How would that be? I believe that all of these predator priests were already predators or at least oriented toward acting out their predatory obsessions when they became priests. The priesthood didn't create predators. It attracted them and protected them.

As disgusting and as sickening as it would be to do it, I would dedicate another entire book to getting to the bottom of these questions. So once again I call upon all of the predatory priests on this planet to contact me and tell me your stories. We all need to understand what happened. Here are more of my unanswered questions. I want and need answers to all of them:

How many priests have sexually abused children and adolescents?

How many sexual abusers are still priests in good standing?

How many of them are bishops or cardinals?

Was a pope ever a sexual abuser?

How many children and adolescents were sexually abused by Catholic priests in the last fifty years?

How many in the last 2,000 years?

Was it a mortal sin for Blessed Pope John Paul II to cover up the sex abuse scandal?

Did he ever confess the sin?

If he did, what was his penance?

Was it more than three Hail Mary's, three Our Father's and three Glory Be's?

To all of the predator priests:

When did you first know that you were a predator?

When did you begin abusing children?

Were you abused by a priest when you were young?

Why did you become a priest?

Were you primarily interested in having access to children?

How did you know that the church would cover up your predation?

Do you believe in any of the teachings of the Catholic Church?

How do you explain your hypocrisy?

How do you live with yourself?

What would be a just punishment for what you have done?

What do you think happens when you die?

I said in the chapter "Way to Go" that when I think of the tens of thousands of dedicated sisters, brothers, priests and lay people who work tirelessly every day to minister to the poor and hungry and to advocate for peace and equality, it brings a tear to my eye. When I think of the unspeakable atrocities committed against our children and young people by predatory priests, it makes me ashamed to be a human being.

THE OLD SCHOOL CHURCH

LET'S GO RETRO

I was thinking about some of the old school Catholic stuff that I grew up with—stuff you just don't hear much about anymore. How about if we revisit briefly some of these things from back in the day? I'm talking about things like the Latin Mass, the Holy Name Society, novenas, the Nine First Fridays, the Five First Saturdays, the Forty Hours Devotion. How about scapulars, holy medals, missals and holy water? What about pagan babies? How about if we take another look?

What do you say? Let's go old school! Let's go retro!

The Latin Mass: Let's start with something really big: the Latin Mass. I'll bet there are a lot of really smart American high school kids who don't even know what Latin is. Don't know that it's a language. Well it is a language, a dead one. It's amazing to think that until 1965 the Mass was always celebrated in Latin. Vatican II changed that and allowed the Mass to be celebrated in the vernacular, i.e., in the language spoken commonly in the country where the Mass was taking place so that would, of course, be English in the good old USA. This change caused a furor at the time and, believe it or not, the controversy is still going on.

I always thought that a big advantage of the Latin Mass was that you had no idea what the hell the priest was saying, so I was fine with keeping it that way. If that puts me on the conservative side of the debate, well then fine. But most of the people who wanted to keep the

Mass in Latin had other reasons. Actually a group called Congregatio Mariae Reginae Immaculatae—the Religious Congregation of Mary Immaculate Queen—pretty much sums up the pro-Latin view. They say it's important for the Mass to be celebrated in Latin, "because it is a dead language. As it is no longer spoken as the vernacular language in any country today, Latin words do not change in meaning." Wow! They like Latin because it is dead and doesn't change. Now you might think, well, the words of the Mass are set by the church, so they don't really change much anyway, right? Well, they don't change often, but they do change from time to time. In fact, Pope Benedict XVI revised the translation of the Mass from the Roman missal, which contains the official Latin version. So what the CMRI guys are saying is they don't ever want the words to change, not ever, ever, ever, and since Latin is dead, you know it will never change. So Latin is good, and the vernacular, the way everybody actually speaks—that's bad. How's that for conservative? Rick Santorum would definitely approve.

In the old school Catholic Church there were all kinds of devotions, which were repetitious practices or prayers focused on some representation of God or Jesus or Mary, the Mother of Jesus, or some particular saint. Here are some examples:

Nine First Fridays: This is something you really don't hear much about any more. If you receive communion on the first Friday of the month nine months in a row, you are showing special devotion to the Heart of Jesus as a sign of his love for human beings. The depiction of the Heart in various paintings is pretty weird. Typically, it's bleeding and bound by a ring of thorns. There's a cross stuck in the top of it, and light is shooting off all around it like fireworks on the Fourth of July. Your reward for devotion to the Heart is that you get all kinds of special blessings and graces.

I was taught by various nuns who were into the Nine First Fridays and that was really bad news. In order to receive communion on the first Friday of the month nine months in a row, you obviously had to go to Mass on the first Friday of the month nine months in a row. That meant being dragged to church not once, but twice, the first week of every month for almost the entire school year.

Novenas: Number 9. Number 9. Number 9. Yes, Yoko, it's another nine-based devotion. Performing a novena means saying special prayers nine days in a row as a special devotion to get special blessings and graces. "Special" is the word! The special devotion can be to the Sacred Heart of Jesus, the Blessed Mother or the saint of your choice. Maybe the church would say otherwise, but I have a hard time believing that many people aside from maybe the CMRI guys who want the Mass to be in Latin are actually doing these nine-based devotions— unless, of course, it's the faithful members of the Holy Name Society.

The Holy Name Society: I don't know how often they met way back then, but when I was a kid, I remember that every once in awhile, after the priest gave a long, boring sermon at Sunday Mass, he would announce an upcoming meeting of the Holy Name Society. Actually the formal name of this group is the Confraternity of the Most Holy Names of God and Jesus. They are devoted to the names of God and Jesus. That's right—devoted to the names. Sounds like lots and lots of praying to me. If this sounds attractive to you, check them out at www.nahns.com.

Other devotions include:

- **The Five First Saturdays:** Focused on the Blessed Mother and kind of like the Nine First Fridays, only it's five and it's Saturday.

- **Thirteen Tuesdays:** Thirteen . . . Tuesdays . . . St. Anthony. If you lost something really important—like maybe one night you were bar hopping and you got really drunk and when you came out of the last bar you had no idea where you parked your car and it's been a few days and you still haven't found it, then the Thirteen Tuesdays are custom-made for you.

- **The Forty Hours Devotion:** Involves venerating the Blessed Sacrament, which is a very thin wafer of unleavened bread stuck inside a gold case that's left out on the altar for almost two days. In other words you're staring at a piece of flat bread in a gold and glass case.

Ash Wednesday: It's the first day of Lent, and the point of Ash Wednesday is to remind us that we'll all be dead one day. Personally, I don't need reminding of that, but I do need reminding of when Ash Wednesday comes each year since it moves around just like Easter. Ash Wednesday always was, and always will be, a big deal in the church, but what makes it totally old school are those ashes. You go to church on Ash Wednesday to get ashes smudged on your forehead supposedly in the shape of a cross although usually it just looks like you wiped your hand on your forehead after changing the oil on your car. If you walk around with the Ash Wednesday smudge on your head all day wherever you go—work, the grocery store, the gym, wherever—you are definitely letting everybody know you are an old school Roman Catholic. Good for you! Let it all hang out!

Lent: It's the period, lasting about six weeks, leading up to Easter when we're all supposed to meditate on how sinful we are and do penance. So Lent is intrinsically old school. After all, there is nothing more old-school Catholic than guilt and sin. A lot of people give up stuff or try to during Lent—like smoking or alcohol or sweets—as a penance for their sins. But maybe the most old school thing about Lent is that you can't eat meat on Ash Wednesday or on any Friday in Lent. OK, but is it still a mortal sin if you do? I hope so because it wouldn't be fair to all of the baloney lovers in Hell—not that they should be in Hell anyway—but it just wouldn't be fair if all of the meat-eating slackers today got a lighter sentence.

Stations of the Cross: This devotion can be performed any time anywhere, even online—isn't the Internet great? But it is most often performed, even staged—sometimes with school kids—during Lent, particularly on Good Friday, in church. A lot of times school kids will even act out the different parts in a kind of pageant. There are fourteen stations, each describing an event in the passion and death of Jesus. Typically, you stop before a depiction of each event and meditate on its meaning. Sometimes the Resurrection is added in as a fifteenth station even though it's not one. I think that's maybe to cheer everybody up.

Sacramentals: These are a whole bunch of different blessed actions and objects that supposedly show respect and veneration for the sacraments. Actually it's kind of hard to get your arms around what sacramentals really are precisely because there are so many of them and they seem to be really different from one another. For example, giving "alms" to the poor and saying the prayer, the Confiteor, which is said at Mass and in which you confess your sins to God; the Blessed Mother; Michael, the Archangel; the apostles, Peter and Paul; all of the saints—and then everybody else who's there—are sacramentals. So are holy water and a whole host of blessed things—candles, ashes, incense, oil, palms, food, scapulars, holy medals, rosaries, crucifixes, pictures, statues, holy cards. That's a partial list. Basically, anything that's blessed is a sacramental. The best blessing of all is of course from the pope.

If you are into sacramentals, you are definitely old-school Catholic. You're also old-school superstitious. I know the church vehemently denies that belief in the power of sacramentals is the same as superstition, but the church clearly believes that sacramentals help keep evil away. In fact, *The Catholic Encyclopedia* says that "one of the most remarkable effects of sacramentals is the virtue to drive away evil spirits whose mysterious and baleful operations affect sometimes the physical activity of man." By "evil spirits" the Encyclopedia guys mean the devil and other demons. OK. So how is believing that holy water and a crucifix ward off demons any different from believing that a rabbit's foot or throwing salt over your shoulder gives you good luck and keeps bad luck away? Empirically, I mean. Well, the difference, according to the church, of course, is that God and Mary and the angels and the saints are really the ones responsible for keeping away the bad guys, and they'll do that for you if you show appropriate devotion to them through your veneration of the blessed objects, whereas there's nobody there on the other side of that rabbit's foot to help you, so if you depend on a rabbit's foot, the demons will get you anyway. Again, if you believe in the power of all of this holy paraphernalia, you are definitely old school, but sorry, you are also superstitious.

Sacramentals are available just about everywhere. One good place to get them is at www.sacramentals.com. You can get a set of 29 holy cards for $12 plus shipping and tax. A 9" x 11" plaque of the Mother of Good Counsel of Genazzano will set you back $40 plus shipping and tax. www.sacramentals.com accepts PayPal or credit cards.

Scapulars: Collecting scapulars could actually be a hobby in it-self. A monastic scapular is a garment that monks and nuns wear over their heads. It hangs down in the front and back. But a devotional scapular is a kind of cloth necklace that comes in different colors and that reflects your devotion to Jesus, the Blessed Mother or maybe your favorite saint. The Brown Scapular of Our Lady of Mount Carmel is maybe the most popular scapular of all. As I mentioned previously, when the Blessed Mother appeared to St. Simon Stock, she told him that if you die while wearing the scapular you go straight to heaven. So the brown scapular of Our Lady of Mount Carmel is viewed by Cath-olics as a "passport to heaven," which is how www.sacramentals.com describes it. That makes the scapular quite a bargain. You actually can purchase eternal salvation for just $6.50 at www.sacramentals.com. They offer a variety of designs, too. In addition to the basic cord ver-sion, you can get it with a heavy white cord or with a holy medal added. If you're a fan of the crusades, you can buy a specially designed "Crusader" version. www.sacramentals.com also offers a host of other attractive scapulars, including brown scapulars of St. Therese, St. Michael the Archangel, St. Padre Pio, St. Maximilian Kolbe (the pa-tron saint of the addicted), Our Lady of Gaudalupe and Our Lady of Fatima. They also have the black scapulars of the Seven Dolors and the Sorrowful Mother, the purple scapular of St. Joseph, the blue scapular of the Immaculate Conception, the green scapular of the Immacu-late Heart of Mary and the white Trinity scapular with a red and blue cross.

If you're really into scapulars, I suggest wearing them outside your shirt or blouse. Even more than walking around with ashes on your forehead all day on Ash Wednesday, external scapular wearing really makes the statement that you are old school Catholic.

Pagan Babies: Back in the day, when I was in grade school, if you gave a penny or a nickel to help out children in developing countries, those children were called "Pagan Babies." Now you just can't get any more old school than that!

THE BALTIMORE CATECHISM

The Baltimore Catechism seems to have the answer to everything or at least to all of the questions that it asks itself. But even more striking than having all of the answers is the tone of the answers. The tone basically says that all of these answers come straight from God, the one true God. There is a finality to every answer that is simply breathtaking. The doctrine of infallibility, however absurd, supposedly applies only to the pope and only when he is speaking on matters of faith and morals—right? It's only in those two instances, which of course basically sum up the whole theological shooting match. But the catechism seems to think that it's infallible, too. There is very definitely an *ex cathedra* feel and attitude to the book.

Now despite the tone, I have to say that the catechism leaves a lot of unanswered questions. It also makes certain assumptions and draws certain conclusions that could not have come directly from God because unfortunately they just aren't true or at least they raise more questions than they answer. Here are some of the unanswered questions that the catechism raises as well as some of the points of view that it fails to consider. The catechism introduces each question with a "Q" and each answer with an "A." I'll introduce each unanswered question with a "UQ" and each unconsidered point of view with a "UPOV." Here we go:

Q: Who is God? A: God is the Creator of heaven and earth, and of all things.

UPOV: That means that he made all of the bad and nasty stuff too—like the Ebola, E. coli and HIV viruses. Bacteria, anyone? You can touch more than thirty bacteria-ridden surfaces or substances in under a minute. Hundreds of different kinds of bacteria are crawling all over me, and they're crawling all over you, too. I know some of them do good things, but I'm sorry. It's just too creepy.

Q: Why did God make you? A: God made you to know Him, to love Him, and to serve Him in this world, and to be happy with Him forever in the next.

UQ: Why does God want to be served? Or is it a need?

Q: What must we do to save our souls? A: To save our souls, we must worship God through faith, hope, and charity; that is, we must believe in Him, hope in Him, and love Him with all our heart.

UQ: Why does God put us in the position of having to save our souls in the first place? Why doesn't he just make sure that our souls are safe? After all, he made us and our souls. Why does God want to be worshipped? Why does God care whether we believe in him or not? Why doesn't he just believe in himself? Why is God looking for our love? Why is he so needy?

UPOV: Maybe God should seek counseling.

Q: Does God see us? A: God sees us and watches over us.

UQ: Is he watching over all of the people who get killed in natural disasters? How about automobile accidents and plane crashes? Is he watching when we have sex? Does that make him a voyeur or a Peeping Tom?

UPOV: Maybe natural disasters occur while God is distracted or maybe when he blinks. Or maybe he's just asleep at the wheel.

Q: *Does God know all things?* **A:** *God knows all things, even our most secret thoughts, words and actions.*

UQ: Doesn't that make God the thought police?

UPOV: That's really disturbing. I value my privacy.

Q: *Can God do all things?* **A:** *God can do all things, and nothing is hard or impossible to Him.*

UQ: Then he could cure all diseases, right?

UPOV: I guess he doesn't want to.

Q: *Is God just, holy, and merciful?* **A:** *God is all just, all holy, and all merciful, and He is infinitely perfect.*

UQ: Then why is the world that he created so screwed up in some many ways?

UPOV: Don't tell me that's because Adam and Eve, two fairy tale characters, ate a piece of fruit. I need a better explanation than that.

Also, don't tell me it's my fault. I wasn't around at the creation of the world. God says he was and that everything was his infinitely perfect idea. God likes to blame people. He should look in the mirror every once in a while and take responsibility himself.

Q: Who were the first man and woman? A: The first man and woman were Adam and Eve.

UPOV: I really wish that the catechism guy were joking here.

Q: What evil befell us through the disobedience of our first parents? A: Through the disobedience of our first parents we all inherit their sin and punishment, as we should have shared in their happiness had they remained faithful.

UPOV: Whoa! Hold on there, pal! You're saying that the fate of hundreds of billions of people throughout all of history depended upon whether or not two people did what they were supposed to do. If they did, everything would have been great, but since they didn't, we have suffering and death, we're all born in sin, liable to go to hell, and so on and so forth. Sorry, but that's the most unjust idea I have ever heard of. In fact, that's way beyond unjust—to borrow a favorite word of the catechism, that's *infinitely* unjust. I had nothing to do with those two naked assholes in the Garden. In fact, if I had been there and I had run into a talking serpent who told me to eat some strange fruit, I would have said, you first, motherfucker.

Q: When was Christ born? A: Christ was born on Christmas Day in a stable in Bethlehem.

UPOV: I'm not trying to be mean, but once again I really wish the catechism guy was joking. Does he actually say Jesus was born on Christmas Day? Yes, he does. First of all, isn't that sort of like me saying I was born on my birthday? But it's worse that that. I guess just want to slap the guy and say, Hey, dude, Christmas Day is just the day that we picked to celebrate Jesus' birth. We have no fucking idea what day he was born.

*Q: What do you mean by the near occasions of sin? **A:** By the near occasions of sin I mean the persons, places, and things that may easily lead us into sin.*

UQ: Does that include the Sunset Strip Lounge in Detroit, Michigan, and Sunny Dee-Lite's parties in Manhattan??

*Q: What is an Indulgence? **A:** An Indulgence is the remission in whole or in part of the temporal punishment due to sin.*

UQ: Is the church still offering a "Buy One, Get One Free" sale on plenary indulgences? Can I buy a plenary indulgence online?

*Q: What is the Sacrament of Matrimony? **A:** The Sacrament of Matrimony is the Sacrament that unites a Christian man and woman in lawful marriage.*

UPOV: Marriage equality, anyone?

*Q: What is holy water? **A:** Holy water is water blessed by the priest with solemn prayer to beg God's blessing on those who use it, and protection from the powers of darkness.*

UQ: Why not just carry a rabbit's foot?

Q: What is forbidden by the Second Commandment? A: The Second Commandment forbids . . . blasphemy, cursing, and profane words.

UPOV: Fuck that.

Q: What are we commanded by the Fourth Commandment? A: We are commanded by the Fourth Commandment to honor, love and obey our parents in all that is not sin.

UQ: Does that mean that you have to agree to an arranged marriage? Can your parents pick your major for you in college? What if they want you to turn over your paycheck to them when you get a job? My father's parents made him do that.

UPOV: Everybody has to earn respect, including parents.

Q: Are we bound to obey others than our parents? A: We are also bound to honor and obey our bishops, priests, magistrates, teachers, and other lawful authorities.

UQ: Say what? Does the catechism guy mean Roman magistrates or judges in small claims court? Are these all examples of lawful authorities? There's no law in the US that says you have to obey bishops, priests and teachers. Who exactly is a lawful authority? The lawful authorities in the US are for the most part elected officials who are supposed to serve the public and if they don't, they can get voted out.

UPOV: Don't follow what the so-called lawful authorities tell you, think for yourself.

Q: What is forbidden by the Sixth Commandment? A: The Sixth Commandment forbids . . . all immodesty with ourselves or others in looks, dress, words, or actions.

UPOV: It's my dick, and I'll touch it if I want to. If somebody else wants to touch it that's up to me, too. Furthermore, if you got it, flaunt it.

Q: Does the Sixth Commandment forbid the reading of bad and immodest books and newspapers? A: The Sixth Commandment does forbid the reading of bad and immodest books and newspapers.

UPOV: The Sixth Commandment appears to be in conflict with the First Amendment to the Constitution of the United States. However, the People's Republic of China would approve.

Q: What are we commanded by the Ninth Commandment? A: We are commanded by the Ninth Commandment to keep ourselves pure in thoughts and desires.

UPOV: The church wants to control your brain and your genitals.

Q: Are we obliged to contribute to the support of our pastors? A: We are obliged to contribute to the support of our pastors, and to bear our share in the expenses of the church and school.

UPOV: And let's not forget about controlling your wallet, too.

I think that about sums it up, so I'll stop there.

Just thinking of all of those unanswered questions and unconsidered points of view almost makes me wish I could go back to Our Lady of Fatima parochial school for just one day, raise my hand during catechism class, and say, "Sister, I have a few questions of my own that I'd like to ask and a couple of thoughts to share, too." I can't even imagine how much trouble I'd be in.

Postscript to *The Baltimore Catechism*: In 2011 the Catholic Church published *Youcat*, a new catechism for young people. The book includes a preface written by Pope Benedict XVI and appears in twenty-five different languages. With a look and feel that is at times reminiscent of a summer camp brochure, the book apparently tries to present a kinder and gentler catechism aimed at drawing youth into the loving embrace of the church. However, the anti-gay sentiment of the book and its distortions of how homosexual people view their sexual orientation expose the artifice of this approach.

The catechism states with extreme awkwardness, "God made man in such a way that he is male or female." Does it really say, "he" is "male or female"? Yes, it does—while asserting that man "longs for fulfillment and completion in the opposite sex." Needless to say, the catechism fails to mention that God made transgender people, too.

Youcat then asks itself, "What about people who feel they are homosexual?" implying that identifying oneself as homosexual may be just a feeling, i.e., delusional or self-generated. The catechism then restates the church's position that because the purpose of sex is procreation, "homosexual practices cannot be approved by the church." But it goes even further, proclaiming the utter absurdity that gay people really wish they were straight. Indeed, *Youcat* avers "that it is a painful experience for many homosexually oriented people that they do not feel erotically attracted to the opposite sex and necessarily miss out on the physical fruitfulness between man and woman according to human nature and the divine order of creation." What a mouthful of made-up garbage! Gay people are pained that they are perverts who can't make babies. Really? If you believe that, young people of the world, then you may be occupying the same alternative universe as Pope Benedict XVI and the *Yucat* authors, and *Youcat* may be the perfect catechism for you. Have fun at summer camp!

The Legion of Decency

The Catholic Legion of Decency was founded in 1933. Its mission was to identify and oppose films that the Catholic Church viewed as morally objectionable. Catholics were encouraged to join the Legion of Decency, to take the Legion of Decency pledge and to renew the pledge once a year. Here's the pledge: "In the name of the Father and of the Son and of the Holy Ghost. Amen. I condemn all indecent and immoral motion pictures, and those which glorify crime or criminals. I promise to do all that I can to strengthen public opinion against the production of indecent and immoral films, and to unite with all who protest against them. I acknowledge my obligation to form a right conscience about pictures that are dangerous to my moral life. I pledge myself to remain away from them. I promise, further, to stay away altogether from places of amusement which show them as a matter of policy."

Films were given one of three ratings, A, B or C:

- **A:** Morally unobjectionable
- **B:** Morally objectionable in part
- **C:** Condemned by the Legion of Decency

The **A** rating was subsequently divided into four different ratings:

- **A-I:** Suitable for all audiences
- **A-II:** Suitable for adults and adolescents

- **A-III:** Suitable for adults only
- **A-IV:** Suitable for adults with reservations

In its heyday the Legion of Decency had tremendous power. If your film was condemned, it was like getting an X rating and your distribution and your potential audience would be dramatically reduced. *A Streetcar Named Desire* and *The Seven Year Itch* were both edited to avoid being condemned.

Incredibly, one of the first films that the Legion of Decency condemned was *Miracle on 34th Street*. That's right. The beloved Santa Claus movie was condemned because it presented a positive view of a divorced woman. Over the years the Legion of Decency condemned numerous Oscar award-winning films including:

- Some Like It Hot
- Spartacus
- Psycho
- Never on Sunday
- 8½
- Rosemary's Baby
- The Last Picture Show
- Carrie
- All That Jazz

For the record the Legion of Decency also condemned *The Odd Couple*—sorry Oscar and Felix—and *The Rocky Horror Picture Show* (transvestites, no good!).

Today the work of the Legion of Decency is continued by the United States Conference of Catholic Bishops Office for Film & Broadcasting and is available through the Catholic News Service. Check out their website at www.catholicnews.com/movies.htm. The condemned rating is now an "O" and stands for morally offensive. Some recent films rated O include *The 40-Year-Old Virgin, Bridesmaids, Brokeback Mountain, Borat!, Date Movie, The Da Vinci Code, Gulliver's Travels. The Hangover, The Hangover Part II, Larry the Cable Guy: Health Inspector, Miami Vice, Religulous, Scary Movie 4 and 5, Scream 4, Sex and the City, Sex and the City 2* and *Wedding Crashers.*

Get Outta Here!

Excommunicated. That's what it's called when you get kicked out of the Catholic Church. No matter what I do, I can't get excommunicated from the Catholic Church. I excommunicated myself a long time ago. I believe that you should always quit a job before you get fired. And that goes for religion, too. It's sort of a take-this-religion-and-shove-it attitude. I have, however, committed excommunicable crimes. These include the following:

1. Apostasy, i.e., rejecting every single belief of the Catholic Church. If you just reject one, you're a heretic. If you reject them all, you're an apostate. I'm an apostate.

2. Schism: This means that you reject that the pope is the head of the church. As I point out in the very first chapter of this book, I think the basis for believing that the pope is the leader of the church of Jesus is very shaky indeed. He is the head of his church. I'm just not sure it has that much to do with Jesus.

3. Abortion: If you have an abortion or you help someone have an abortion, you are automatically excommunicated. In 2010 Sister Margaret McBride was excommunicated for advising a young woman who was eleven weeks pregnant and suffering from a life-threatening condition to have an abortion to save her life. Sister Margaret provided the advice as a member of the ethics

committee of St. Joseph's Hospital and Medical Center in Phoenix. Some Catholics take this issue even further and believe that that if you are pro-choice, you should be excommunicated. That would be me. Clearly, women have reproductive rights. They have the right to choose to continue a pregnancy or have an abortion. No one has the right to force a woman to have a child.

4. Getting divorced and then getting married again: I did that. Then I got married and divorced a second time. I was also engaged to another woman for three weeks after that, but that's another story. OK. In this case you used to get excommunicated, but then the church changed its mind, and now you're not excommunicated. Now, if you get divorced and then get married again, you just can't receive communion. You also can't be buried in a Catholic cemetery. Bummer!

5. Here's one that's kind of borderline: You are excommunicated if you hear a confession and you're not a priest. I've never actually heard a confession. I'm not a priest, and I can't imagine that anybody would want to confess their sins to me, but there does exist a photograph of me sitting in the priest's part of the confessional box in a church somewhere in Italy making the sign of the cross to absolve an invisible penitent of his sins.

Interestingly, you are not excommunicated for the following crimes:

1. Committing genocide: That would have ex-ed out all of the Crusades guys. Of course, popes and saints, such as Pope Urban II and St. Louis (King Louis IX), were the ones behind the holy slaughter to begin with.

2. Torture, as in the various Inquisitions.

3. Witch-Hunts, as in murdering innocent women by burning them at the stake.

4. Anti-Semitism—Hello there, St. John Chrysostom, St. Hippolytus and St. Cyril, to name just a few anti-Semitic saints.

5. Religious intolerance, as in labeling anybody who is not a Christian an infidel (who have I heard using that word lately? Oh, yeah. That would be the radical Islamists.) also, labeling non-Catholic Christians as heretics.

6. Being an anti-gay, anti-lesbian, anti-transgender bigot.

7. Hypocrisy, hello all of you anti-gay gay priests.

8. Sexual abuse of children and teenagers—what can you say about the greatest disgrace of all? Hey, those guys are all still Catholics and they're all still priests—after all, once a priest, always a priest, right?

And that's the point. You can do all of these things and still be a Catholic, still be a priest—the representative of Jesus Christ on earth. So you realize that excommunication is all about enforcing orthodoxy. It has nothing to do with whether you're a good or a bad person. You can be a monster and still be a Catholic in good standing. You can be a compassionate and ethical person, like Sister Margaret, who has no doubt dedicated her life to the church, and be shown the church door.

HYPOCRISY

Hypocrisy and the Catholic Church. It's like peanut butter and jelly, soup and sandwich, bagels and lox. Inseparable. Most institutions are hypocritical, certainly most churches. It's just that the Catholic Church is so good at it, and there can only be one number one. When it comes to hypocrisy, the Catholic Church wins hands down. Once again, when I say "the Catholic Church," I mean the priests and bishops, the church's leadership, not the one billion or so Catholics who do or don't follow them.

Let's just give a few examples of why the Catholic Church is the gold standard for hypocrisy here on planet earth.

Hypocrisy Proof Point Number 1—Homosexuality: I cover this in greater detail in "In the Closet," but let me make my point here again somewhat differently. The Catholic Church is either the gayest straight organization or the straightest gay organization in the world. Even the straight priests wear dresses, and the pope looks like he bought out Liberace's closet in an estate sale. The only organization I know of that has a higher percentage of gay membership than Catholic priests is the Gay Men's Health Crisis.

So the Catholic Church is just loaded to the gills with closeted gay men, and, as we all know—drum roll please—it's anti-gay. Totally. The Catholic Church says that homosexuality is "disordered." So all you gay guys at the Republican National Committee, please straighten your bow ties.

According to the Catholic Church, homosexuality is contrary to natural law. (Aside: Could you explain natural law to me, Brian Greene or Michio Kaku, using string theory, I mean? I'm just not clear on how it works, particularly at quantum levels.) According to the church, any homosexual attraction is "disordered," i.e., in a state of high entropy, because it draws one to engage in a homosexual act, and a homosexual act is—drum roll again, please—sinful. Right. God doesn't like cock sucking or butt fucking. No girl on girl either. For him it's peanut butter and jelly, soup and sandwich, bagels and lox, cock and pussy.

Now In fairness to the church, all of this cock and pussy stuff is pretty simple to keep track of. Follow me boys and girls, because it goes like this: if you want to fuck, you have to get married first, and the person you marry has to be of the opposite sex. So if you're a boy, you need to marry a girl, and if you're a girl, you need to marry a boy. One little wrinkle: Transgender people please refer to the genitalia you were born with; if they're no longer there, I'm afraid you're out of luck. Once you're married, it's actually OK to fuck, but, guys, make sure that every drop of your sperm is deposited neatly in the vagina that you are married to. Otherwise, you and your wife just committed a mortal sin even though you went to all of the trouble to marry each other before you finally got down to fucking.

Hypocrisy Proof Point Number 2—Sex Abuse Scandal: The Catholic church states that it is the one, true church. It states that the Pope is the Vicar of Christ. The church says that it represents Jesus on earth. In fact, the church says that every single priest represents Jesus on earth and has the power to forgive sins in his name, and yet thousands of priests sexually abused children and adolescents. Raped them. Preyed upon them. And these predator priests were allowed by their colleagues and their pastors and their bishops and their popes to continue their predation with impunity.

When a priest was exposed as a child molester, he was not turned over to the police. He was not even relieved of his priestly duties and isolated from the defenseless children and adolescents that he was bent on preying upon. No. Instead he was reassigned to another unsuspecting parish or school where he was allowed to resume his predation and rape.

Thousands of priests across the globe were guilty of this unspeakable crime and the church denied it, covered it up and obstructed investigations about it for decades. Again, it was fellow priests and pastors and bishops and popes who looked the other way and denied the truth and lied to protect rapists and child molesters. Blessed Pope John Paul II did it, too.

For shame. Shame on the church. The church loves the concept of eternity. Well, good. The shame of this church is eternal. This shame will never go away.

Hypocrisy Proof Point Number 3—Mary and the Denigration of Women: Mary, the Mother of Jesus, is the best person who ever lived except for Jesus, and he had to be God to beat her. Mary is so good, she was immaculately conceived, which means that she was born without original sin. So the fruit-eating debacle in the Garden of Eden didn't even touch her. Mary was also able to conceive Jesus, give birth to him and still be a virgin. That is truly amazing. I wish that birth had been captured on video and put up on YouTube. I'd like to see how the heck Jesus got out. Anyway, what all this adds up to is that Mary is perfect. She is elevated above all other human beings (again, except for her Son), and she is (gasp!) a woman. Well, sort of. She's more like a goddess. Nevertheless, this means that the greatest person of all time was a woman while at the same time—according to the church—all other women, all 60 or so billion women who were ever born, are unworthy. They are inferior to men; they are subordinate to men; they can't be priests; they can't be leaders of the church, and at least according to St. Paul, they should wear a hat and shut the fuck up when they're in church.

What a grotesque disparity! Mary is the greatest, and all other women are subordinate to men. Now in fairness to the church, they say it's not their fault. God set things up this way. He's the one who made women subordinate to men, inferior to men, and he's the one who won't let the church ordain women. So don't blame the church for treating women like shit. They're just following orders. Holy Orders, that is. The orders are direct from God, and until they get a new set of orders (I guess it's sort of like the army), they, the men, will have to keep on running everything, and the women will have to keep on wearing hats and zipping their lips in church—except of course when it's time to sing a hymn like "Hail Holy Queen Enthroned Above" or "Ave Maria."

Hypocrisy Proof Point Number 4—Annulment: As we all know, Jesus said, "What therefore God has joined together, let not man separate." (Mark 10: 9) What he actually meant to say was, "What therefore God has joined together, let not man separate," unless you're in with the guy who heads up your Diocesan Tribunal and can cough up the right amount of money." Example: I know a woman who is the best person ever, right after Mary, a devout Catholic, married by a priest in church. After being married for eighteen years to the biggest asshole in the world and after having four children, the asshole wanted to ditch her for another woman. Guess what? The asshole went to this very understanding diocesan tribunal guy, and he got an annulment. Just like that—no problem at all.

An annulment means you were never really married. Say what! Yes, you were never really married even if you were married by a priest in church, were supposedly married for eighteen years and had four children. The whole thing was an illusion. You were never married at all.

In this case, the asshole married the woman he was cheating with, and they're both Catholics in good standing and receive communion at Mass every week.

This happened a number of years ago, so the price was only five grand. I'm sure it's gone up since then, but hey, whatever the price, it's a bargain to be able to wipe away the reality of eighteen years of marriage, and say they never happened and then get married again—sorry, for the first time—and still be a Catholic in good standing. That's almost like magic, isn't it? And magic, like hypocrisy, is priceless.

NOTHING BUT QUESTIONS

Hurts So Good

Question: Why is suffering good? Apparently because God likes it. Maybe he likes it so much because it was his idea in the first place. He didn't have to create a world in which there was suffering, but he did.

I wonder what God's favorite form of suffering is. For example, when it comes to natural disasters, does he prefer earthquakes or tsunamis? What's more entertaining—famine or epidemic? Terminal diseases are really hard to beat when it comes to suffering. Of course, that's just here on earth. On a cosmic level does he prefer Black Holes that suck entire galaxies filled with populated planets into oblivion, or do exploding supernovas get his mojo working even more? I'm sure he's really looking forward to the final collapse of the universe, assuming there's enough matter to reverse the currently accelerating expansion and reduce the entire universe to the size of a Planck length.

Is there maybe a fantasy disaster league where God and the angels and the devils and maybe some of God's favorite saints like the Jew-hating St. John Chrysostom and St. Dominic, the Inquisition guy, get to compete on what earthly disasters kill the most people in a given year? Of course, God would have to participate in just a kind of joking, I'm-just-fucking-with-you sort of way, since of course he already knows who's going to die and how.

We know God loves suffering. When he got really upset about how the human beings that he created were behaving, he decided that the only thing that would make him feel better was to send his son, Jesus, who was really just another version of himself, down to earth to be tortured and die. So it was either the murder of his son or some weird form of suicide that succeeded in cheering up the Creator of the Universe, enabling him to get over his anger at the human race.

That's why the Catholic Church teaches that suffering brings you closer to God, closer to Jesus. This was a favorite idea of Mother Teresa. She was a big fan of suffering. She devoted her life to taking in the poor, the sick and the homeless and then refusing to give them pain medication. I'll bet that was a surprise to all of the terminally ill people who were in excruciating pain. But they needed to understand that the good Mother was just helping them get closer to Jesus before they died.

Aside from allowing you to get closer to Jesus, suffering is redemptive, too. That means if you suck it up and don't whine and offer up your suffering to God, he reduces the time you have to burn in purgatory for sins that you confessed and he forgave. If you offer up your suffering for the people who are currently burning in purgatory, he might reduce a tiny bit of their time, too.

Suffering is, of course, central to the whole idea of self-denial. Why is self-denial good? Well, that's because the "self" is bad. That means you and me. We're bad. What we want to do is bad. So we need to deny ourselves, do what we don't want to do. Do the opposite. If you're hungry, don't eat. If you're thirsty, don't drink. You like to be comfortable? Wear a hair shirt. You might also want to consider following the example of Blessed Pope John Paul II. Keep a special belt in the closet, and every once in a while when you're feeling a little complacent, take it out and beat the shit out of yourself. I mean really beat yourself until you bleed and have welts all over your body. Basically you should flagellate yourself until it looks like you were in a really nasty car wreck. I guarantee you won't feel complacent after doing that.

This practice of starving yourself and dehydrating yourself and wearing a hair shirt and beating the shit out of yourself is called "mortification of the flesh," which literally means putting the flesh to death. This is central to self-denial, because the flesh is really the worst part of the self. You need to die to it, or it needs to die to you—the sooner the better. If you're really good at mortifying your flesh, you might even be blessed with the stigmata. That means that your hands and your feet start bleeding all by themselves, and you end up with infected open sores that look like the wounds Jesus had from being nailed to the cross. If this doesn't happen by itself, you can always just create the wounds yourself. Just dig away at the palms of your hands and the top of your feet with a really disgusting rusty nail, and the stigmata will appear soon enough. In fact, your stigmata will look just as good as if it had appeared all by itself, and people will be extremely impressed with how holy you are. There's really good precedent for doing this, too, since it's undoubtedly what people like St. Francis of Assisi and St. Padre Pio did to get their stigmata. And if anybody dares to call you a fraud, just remember that you are following in the footsteps of two of the greatest saints in the history of the church.

Of course, all of the great saints understood the importance of suffering and the spiritual value of self-denial. As I've discussed, in his books on purgatory and hell Fr. Schouppe provides countless examples of saints who perform truly unbelievable acts of mortification and self-denial. He emphasizes that one of the best ways to avoid sin is not only to meditate constantly on the horrors of hell but to try to simulate the experience of hell, especially when we are tempted to sin. He relates the story of St. Martinian, who lived in total solitude for twenty-five years. One day, out of the blue, there was a knock at the door of Martinian's solitary cell. It appeared to be a beggar woman, so Martinian let her in. In reality the woman was not a beggar but a prostitute by the name of Zoe. For reasons that I can never hope to comprehend, Zoe had gotten it into her head that she wanted to fuck Martinian. As soon as she got in the door, Zoe stripped off her beggar clothes and presented herself in the wondrous attire of a courtesan. She must have presented a terrible temptation to Martinian, who may not have even seen a woman for a couple of decades. Nevertheless, the undoubtedly beautiful and sexy Zoe was no match for Martinian. He had the perfect plan for avoiding sexual temptation. After taking one look at Zoe, he took off his shoes and plunged his feet into the fire that was burning in the hearth. Martinian screamed with pain, but he considered the weak earthly fire to be nothing in comparison to the fire that he would be subjected to in hell if he were to give in to fleshly temptation. This act of extreme self-mortification not only enabled Martinian to reject sin, but Zoe was so impressed by Martinian's burning feet that she gave up her career as a sex worker and converted right on the spot.

Now you can't stick your feet into a fire every day of the week to mortify your flesh. In fact, you may not be able to do it more than once. But the saints have shown us that there are many ways to practice self-denial and to mortify our flesh for the greater glory of God. I've already mentioned starving yourself, dehydration, wearing a hair shirt, beating the shit out of yourself and producing the stigmata with a rusty nail (by the way, acid does a pretty good stigmata job, too). Here are some more favorite self-mortification practices that have been tested and approved by some of the greatest saints in the Catholic Church:

- To avoid sexual temptation here are some things that saints have done, (unlike Martinian's foot-in-the-fire routine, you can do these things more than once): St. Francis of Assisi rolled in the snow; St. Benedict threw himself into a thorn bush; St. Bernard jumped into an icy pond.

- I already mentioned starving yourself, but here's a really good twist on that idea: St. Catherine of Siena lived on nothing but the Holy Eucharist for long periods of time.

- In addition to wearing a hair shirt, St. Ignatius of Loyola wore a heavy chain—sort of like the ghost of Jacob Marley—and also tied himself up with a cord below the knees.

- St. John-Baptiste-Marie Vianney had lots of good self-mortification ideas: he would go without sleep; when he did sleep it was never in a bed but on a mattress or on the floor in the attic or maybe even on top of a pile of wood in the basement; he would curb his curiosity by never reading a newspaper; he deprived himself of the pleasure of smelling flowers; and if a fly was bothering him, he would just let it keep on bothering him.

- Many people wear a crucifix as a sign of devotion, but St. Peter Claver wore one that was studded with sharp points.

- As you can see, the possibilities are nearly endless. You can follow the example of these and other saints or come up with your own ideas for self-mortification. It's pretty easy to know if your approach is working. If you become anorexic, dehydrated, sleep-deprived, have infected wounds that won't heal and people look at you as if you are suffering from a severe case of mental illness, then you are definitely on the right track.

LIVIN' ON A PRAYER

Just about everybody believes in God, and just about everybody prays. I don't, but almost everybody else does—well, maybe something like 90 percent, judging from the polls or studies I've seen, which is a pretty high number. It's really hard to get 90 percent of all people lined up together on anything. I'll bet if you took a poll on how many people love their mothers, you wouldn't get 90 percent of them to say "yes," assuming people told the truth. But apparently 90 percent of all people believe in God and pray every day. Hey, that means that just about everybody who believes in God prays to him, too. (Aside: Even though they would probably not be included in these numbers, I wonder how many people who don't believe in God pray anyway just to play it safe.)

Anyway I have a hard time understanding how praying makes any sense whatever the reason for the praying. So I'd like to ask for some help from my readers on this—prayers and non-prayers alike. How about letting me know your thoughts on my thoughts as well as giving me your answers to some of the questions I have. Here we go:

One of the top reasons for praying is to worship God. "Worship" is such a weird concept. Why would you want to worship anybody or anything? The idea seems so primitive and self-denigrating—like you're a serf worshipping the king. And why does God want to be worshipped anyway? Is he insecure? If I were God, I wouldn't want anybody to worship me. I wouldn't need the worship in the first place.

After all, I would be God, and I think I'd lose all respect for all of the brown-nosing, ass-kissing worshippers. I think I would find the whole worship thing to be very tiresome and annoying.

Another big reason for praying is to tell God you're sorry for something you did and that you won't do it any more. First of all, the "I'm sorry" prayer—the so-called "act of contrition"—is really just total bullshit in most cases. Whatever it is that you did, you'll probably do it again. In fact, you'll probably keep on doing it until the day you die. It's part of who you are. Why not accept that and move on? And what's the point of all of the self-flagellation and guilt? What a waste of time! What's more, why does God care about what we do anyway? Doesn't he have better things to do than to get bent out of shape over what you did or didn't do? He's the one who created you in the first place, right? So really he has to accept a lot of the blame for the rotten stuff you do. And since he's supposed to be all knowing, didn't he know that you would do whatever bad thing you did before you were even born?

Thank you, Lord! This is a very popular prayer. If your son's team won a soccer game or you got a raise or maybe you're an asshole recording artist and you just won a Grammy, you thank the Creator of the Universe because you think he made the good thing happen for you. There's just one word to describe that (albeit hyphenated) and that's "self-delusion"—well maybe two words. "Stupidity" works too.

I believe. This is a totally unnecessary prayer. If you know what you believe, and God knows what you believe, why repeat it over and over again?

Ejaculations: Ejaculations are great when they come out of your dick. Not when they come out of your mouth. Talk about repetition! People who repeat stuff like, "My Jesus, mercy," or "Pray, fast and be holy for tomorrow we die," need to get checked for OCD.

Praying for somebody who's sick or for victims of natural disasters: Everybody does this, and it makes no sense whatsoever. If God can intervene and cure somebody who's sick, why did he let them get sick in the first place? Also, isn't he the one who invented the viruses and the bacteria that make everybody sick? It's the same thing with natural disasters. Hurricanes, tsunamis, earthquakes, those are all God's ideas. Isn't it his fault when people are victimized by natural disasters? God kills a bunch of people, and then you pray to him, the killer, to help out the survivors. That's nuts!

Please, God. Please help me! Prayers for help in general make no sense. If God is all-knowing, he knows you're in trouble. If God is all-good, why doesn't he just help you? Why does he always have to be persuaded to help?

Finally, there are people like Michele Bachmann who say they talk to God all of the time, and God answers back. They also claim that God tells them to go out and do certain things, like in Michele's case, it's run for president, although maybe that was God playing a joke on Michele given how all of that worked out. My advice is if you see anybody who claims to be on a first name basis with God coming your way, run!

So that's what I think. Let me know what you think. Email me, tweet me, hit me up on Facebook. Whatever. If you're a prayer, let me know why you worship, why you are always telling God you're sorry, why you're telling him stuff he already knows if he's out there and why you're always trying to persuade God to help you. I'd also like to know how you know when you're prayers are answered. Explain that to me. I'd really like to know.

WHAT'S IT ALL ABOUT?

Does it make any sense to think that the people running the Catholic Church are devoting all of their time and energy trying to make sure we all believe the right things and behave the right way so that everything will work out just fine for us when we're dead? I'll tell you. The answer to that question is a big fat "No!" I'm sorry. I know human beings—after all I do belong to that club—and I can tell you that's not human. Nobody devotes their life to making sure other people are in good shape after they're dead. I can't judge motivation, but I can judge that because that's not a motivation. That's bull shit, so something else is going on.

Of course, what I'm saying doesn't just apply to the people running the Catholic Church. It also applies in varying degrees to the people running other institutional religions as well. Once again, do you really think that any of these people are motivated to do what they do by concern about what happens to you after you're dead? That they want to make sure you're saved from being put in a pizza oven by an all-loving God? If you want to believe that, go right ahead. It's perfectly fine with me. I'm just here to tell you that you are totally deluded.

If this motivation were true, it would be an absolutely superhuman example of altruism. Now what about truly human examples of altruism? Do we have those? Of course, we do. Think of the 911 first responders who charged into the World Trade Center buildings; think of the first responders at the Boston Marathon bombings; think of fire-fighters who are ready to risk their lives every day to save you if your home or office is engulfed in flames; think of the men and women who volunteer for the armed forces and fight wars to protect our security and defend our way of life. I'm talking about the ones who do it to protect lives, not the ones who are naïve, or who just don't have anything better to do, so they enlist. Think of the Navy Seals who went into Osama bin Laden's compound in Pakistan and killed him. Think of the civil rights marchers and the Freedom Riders who risked their lives to oppose racism and discrimination. Those people really acted selflessly. All of these altruists care about you now—when you are alive. They care about keeping you alive and/or making sure that while you are alive you remain free and secure and that your rights are protected. These people are special. There aren't that many of them.

Now, let's consider the people running the Catholic Church and the other institutional religions. What are they up to? Well, I say they're up to what the institution is up to. After all, they're running it. And just what is the institution—the Catholic Church—up to? That's simple. The church is about controlling your brain, your genitals and your wallet. They want to control what you believe and what you think. They want to control when you have sex, who you have sex with, and the kind of sex you have. Last, but not least, they want your money. I would say that once you control those three things—brain, genitals and wallet—you've pretty much wrapped up the whole shooting match. Now that's what I call totalitarian.

The church says, believe what we tell you to believe. We're infallible. We're the one, true church. If you don't believe it, you won't go to heaven. You'll go to hell. You can have sex, but only if you're married. You can only get married if you're straight, so no marriage and no sex if you're gay or transgender. When you do have sex, married man and woman, make sure it's vaginal intercourse; make sure all of the sperm is deposited in the vagina and don't use contraception under any circumstances. That would violate the sanctity of your marriage and is opposed to natural law. Also, if you get pregnant, married lady, make sure you have the baby even if you already have more kids than you can handle and even if the pregnancy might kill you. And oh, yes, please give us your money. Tithing would be nice. Giving even more, giving until it hurts, that would be even nicer.

What's it all about? That's it. Case closed.

I'm not saying that there aren't lots of Catholic priests, nuns and brothers who are good, devoted people doing amazing work all over the world. The same is true of ministers, rabbis, imams, monks and other deputized religious types, as well as the tens of millions of good people who believe in God and are members of a particular religion. That's all true.

But when it comes to the institution and the people running it—in the case of the Catholic Church, that's the priests, bishops, cardinals and, of course, above all the pope—they are about control. They want to control you in this life with the idea that if you do what they say you'll be fine when you're dead. You'll be saved.

Sorry. I don't buy it. It's just plain crazy to believe it, but the craziest thing is just how many people do.

Unanswered Questions

What is the percentage of gay priests?

How many popes were gay?

How many popes have worn panties—not every day but at least once?

How often does the pope go commando?

Do the gay priests really think that it is bad to be gay?

If Vegas were placing over/under odds on the percentage of gay priests, what would it be? (I'm thinking 90 percent.)

When gay guys fuck is it an extra sin for them to wear condoms, or is that only true for straight couples that don't want babies?

Is it a sin to make a contribution to Planned Parenthood?

What is the church's definition of hypocrisy?

What is the total net worth of the Catholic Church?

How much money would the pope's clothing collection raise at auction?

Does the popemobile ever depreciate?

Why doesn't the Catholic Church just give away all of its money to poor people?

If the pope tried to give away all of the church's money to poor people, who would stop him?

Can the pope be fired?

Does anybody still tip their hat when they pass a church?

How many exorcisms does the church perform each year?

What is the average number of devils cast out in each exorcism?

Where do the devils go after they've been cast out?

Are they eligible to file for unemployment?

How did the devils escape from hell in the first place?

Do the devils have names?

Do the devils have photo IDs?

Do their mothers love them?

Are there photographs or videos of the devils?

Do the devils have a right to an attorney?

Would it ever be a good idea to keep a devil as an exotic pet?

Do they bite?

What do they eat?

What was the average daily wage of the workers who built the Cathedrals of Europe?

Were any of them eligible for workman's compensation?

How about disability?

Is it better to adore God or worship him?

Why does God care if you believe in him or not? Why doesn't he just believe in himself?

Why does God take everything so personally?

When I beat off, is God looking, or does he avert His eyes?

Does God really care about who we fuck?

Why does God want to be feared?

Was prayer God's idea?

Is there any information on which prayer God likes best?

What's his favorite hymn?

What's his favorite day of the year—Christmas or Easter?

Can God travel faster than the speed of light?

Is he comfortable hanging out at the event horizon of a Black Hole?

Can God go back in time or visit the future?

What does God do all day?

Does God ever sleep?

Does God ever get bored?

Does God ever get tired of being God?

Does God ever wish that he were somebody else?

Does he ever suffer from low self-esteem?

Has he ever used performance-enhancing drugs?

Would he ever submit to mandatory drug testing?

Does God have a sense of humor?

Is he a fan of ethnic humor?

Are bathroom jokes beneath him?

Does he tell bird jokes when the Holy Spirit isn't around?

Does he think that all of his jokes are funny?

Does anybody have the guts to tell him when his jokes just suck?

Does God ever get silly or maybe do something stupid just for the fuck of it?

Is God good at chess, or does he prefer a relaxing game of checkers?

What about tic-tac-toe?

What happens if it turns out God is gay?

What if God is a woman?

Could God be both a man and a woman?

Is there a rule that God the Father, Jesus and the Holy Spirit have to meet at least once a year?

When they meet, does the Holy Spirit show up as a bird?

When they meet, is anybody else invited, or is the meeting closed to the public?

Are there minutes of the meeting?

If they do meet this year, will they announce a dividend increase or a stock buyback program?

Have they ever had an argument?

Do they ever talk behind each other's backs?

Do all decisions have to be agreed to unanimously, or does a simple majority suffice?

Who's better looking, God the Father or Jesus?

Would the Holy Spirit ever consider appearing as a contestant on the Celebrity Apprentice to revitalize his career?

Would he call Donald Trump, Mr. Trump?

Do Mary and Joseph live together in heaven, or do they maintain separate residences?

How often does Jesus visit them?

What does Jesus give Mary on Mother's Day?

What about Father's Day?

Does Joseph get anything?

If he gets a Father's Day present from Jesus, does the Holy Spirit ever get jealous and steal it from him?

Is Mary still a virgin?

How about Jesus?

When Jesus chose the twelve apostles, did he exclude gays?

Why were there no women apostles?

Does Jesus still keep in touch with the apostles?

Have Jesus and Judas spoken since the betrayal?

Does Jesus still have scars from the crucifixion or have they healed?

Does Jesus get annoyed when saints fake the stigmata?

Does Jesus have any piercings or tattoos?

Does he work out regularly?

Is Mary Magdalene still hot?

After Jesus spent forty days and forty nights in the desert, did he have really bad B.O.?

How was his breath?

Did he have a serious booger problem?

Was even the devil grossed out by his B.O. and bad breath?

Did the devil offer Jesus an Altoid?

Forty days is a long time to be out in the sun. Did Jesus burn or tan?

If you go AWOL from the Blue Army of Our Lady of Fatima and you're caught, what's the punishment?

Is "Don't Ask, Don't Tell" still in force in the Blue Army?

How often should bleeding statues get tested for STDs?

What is the proper etiquette if you/re visited by an angel? Should you offer him a drink? What about cookies and milk, or are they reserved for Santa Claus?

Why is it that all of the angels are men, but they always look like girls or maybe like members of a big hair metal band from the 1980s?

If you're willing to make an extra donation, will the church consider offering a premium altar wine?

Will they allow more than one sip?

When I attended Our Lady of Fatima elementary school back in the sixties, why did they sell a chewy, sugary, black licorice candy, called nigger babies every day at recess? The candy was shaped like a little person, and you could buy two for a penny.

Since Jesus was Jewish, did he take the Church's anti-Semitism personally?

If you see an apparition of Jesus or Mary, how do you know it's Jesus or Mary and not a celebrity look-a-like?

If you die and go to heaven but are really bored, is there any other place to go except purgatory, hell or limbo?

If so, can I book a reservation right now?

Was It a Sin?

When I was growing up, it seemed like almost everything was a sin. It was a sin to have a baloney sandwich on Friday. It was a sin to sleep in and skip Mass on Sunday. It was a sin to touch yourself "in an impure manner." Actually these were really serious sins—mortal sins—and if you died right after you committed them and you to didn't have a second to say, hey, I'm sorry for that baloney sandwich, you went straight to hell.

But thinking about it now, I have to say there were some things that I have questions about. Were they sins or not? Here are a few of the things I have questions about. If you know whether these were sins or not, tweet me @joewenke. If some of them are, I may have to go back and redo a few confessions, you know, kind of take a mulligan (then again the statute of limitations may have run out—after all it's been more than forty years since my last confession):

Was it a sin to wipe the Ash Wednesday ashes off your forehead as soon as you got to the nearest men's room?

Was it a sin to chew the host?

I know it was a sin to say, "Go fuck yourself," because that's nasty, or to say "Goddamn it" or "Jesus Christ" because that's taking the Lord's name in vain, but was it a sin to say any of the following words:

- Poop
- Shit

- Crap
- Bitch
- Bastard
- Jerk Off
- Jack Off
- Ass
- Tits
- Boobs
- Dick
- Prick
- Cock
- Cunt
- Pussy

Note: The nuns back in grade school used to call the big dust balls in the back of the classroom by the coat closet, pussies—I've never figured out why.

And speaking of the nuns: Was it a sin if you had an impure thought about the Mother Superior's panties but then you immediately threw up?

Was it a sin to splash the holy water?

Was it a sin to blow out all of the votive candles, just for fun?

Was it a sin to put *Monopoly* money or money from *The Game of Life* in an envelope and drop it into the collection basket at Sunday Mass? My favorite donation was the white $100,000 bill with a picture of Art Linkletter on it from *The Game of Life*.

Was it a sin to stand behind the altar and do artificial farts under the arm when nobody else was in the church but you?

How about standing on the communion rail and giving the entire empty church the finger?

Was it a sin to sneak into the confession booth and pretend you were the priest hearing confession?

How about moving up the confession line really close to the confessional so you could listen in, especially if there was a hot girl or guy inside?

Was it a sin when you were a teenager and you were out on a date and you tried to feel up your girlfriend's tits, but it turned out she didn't have any?

Finally, is it a sin to touch yourself in an impure manner if you have erectile dysfunction?

* * *

Bibliography

Read on, Brothers and Sisters!

Amorth, Fr. Gabriele. *An Exorcist Tells His Story*. Trans. Nicoletta V. MacKenzie. San Francisco: Ignatius Press, 1999.

Asbridge, Thomas. *The Crusades: The Authoritative History of the War for the Holy Land*. New York: HarperCollins e-books, 2010.

Baltimore Catechism. No. 1-4. Third Plenary Council of Baltimore, 1885-91.

Butler, Alban. *Lives of Saints*. Wyatt North Publishing, 2012.

The Catechism of Saint Pius X (1908). Trans. Right Reverend Monsignor John Hagan for *A Compendium of Catechetical Instruction* (1910). Rpt. Dublin: Browne and Nolan, 1928.

The Complete List of Catholic Saints. Wyatt North Publishing, 2012.

Craughwell, Thomas, J. *Saints Preserved: An Encyclopedia of Relics*. New York: Image Books, 2011.

Duffy, Eamon. *Saints & Sinners: A History of the Popes*. Third Edition. New Haven: Yale University Press, 2006.

Fortea, Fr. José Antonio. *Interview with an Exorcist: An Insider's Look at the Devil, Demonic Possession and the Path to Deliverance.* West Chester, PA: Ascension Press, 2006.

Hardon, John, A., S.J. *The Catholic Catechism.* New York: Image Books, 1981.

Harris, Sam. *Free Will.* New York: Free Press, 2012.

Hitchens, Christopher. *The Missionary Position: Mother Teresa in Theory and Practice.* London and New York: Verso, 1995.

The Holy Bible. English Standard Version. Kindle Edition. Wheaton, IL: Crossway Bibles, 2007.

Maunder, C. J. *Apparitions of the Virgin Mary in Modern European Roman Catholicism (from 1830).* Ph.D. thesis. University of Leeds, 1991.

Murphy, Cullen. *God's Jury: The Inquisition and the Making of the Modern World.* New York: Houghton Mifflin Harcourt, 2012.

O'Malley, John W., S.J., *A History of the Popes: From Peter to the Present.* London: A Sheed & Ward Book, 2010.

Schouppe, F. X., S.J. *The Dogma of Hell: Illustrated by Facts Taken from Profane and Sacred History.* Charlotte, North Carolina: Tan Books, 2010.

Schouppe, F. X., S.J. *Purgatory: Explained by the Lives and Legends of the Saints.* Rockford, IL: Tan Books and Publishers, 1984.

Youcat: Youth Catechism of the Catholic Church. Trans. Michael J. Miller. San Francisco: Ignatius Press, 2010.

Some Cool and Some Not So Cool Websites

www.americancatholic.org

www.ascension-research.org

www.asksistermarymartha.blogspot.com

www.bishop-accountability.org

www.catholic.org

www.catholicapologetics.org

www.catholicbible101.com

www.catholiccompany.com

www.catholicleague.org

www.catholicmodesty.com

www.catholictradition.org

www.catholicvote.org

www.churchsupplywarehouse.com

www.cmri.org

www.couragerc.net

www.directfromlourdes.com

www.documentacatholicaomnia.eu/o1p/1252-05-15%2c_SS_
    Innocentius_IV%2c_Bulla_%27Ad_Extirpanda%27%2c_EN.pdf

www.familycenter.org

www.fisheaters.com

www.fivefirstsaturdays.org

www.fordham.edu/halsall/source/chrysostom-jews6.asp

www.hardonsj.org

www.holymotherchurch.blogspot.com

www.johnthebaptist.us

www.legionariesofchrist.org

www.nahns.com

www.newadvent.com

www.odan.org

www.opusdei.org

www.popebenedictxvifanclub.com

www.praythemass.org

www.priestswithcourage.org

www.quotecatholic.com

www.religious-vocation.com

www.restoredtraditions.com

www.romancatholicism.org

www.sacramentals.com

www.the-american-catholic.com

www.vatileaks.com

www.wdtprs.com

www.womenpriests.org

ABOUT THE AUTHOR

JOE WENKE is a writer, social critic and LGBTQI rights activist. Wenke received a B.A. in English from the University of Notre Dame, an M.A. in English from Penn State and a Ph.D. in English from the University of Connecticut.

Author's photo by Gisele Alicea (aka Gisele Xtravaganza)

PRAISE FOR JOE WENKE'S
YOU GOT TO BE KIDDING!

"A radically funny book." *Christopher Rudolph, The Advocate*

"Gisele, the notable transgender fashion model, graces the cover. And that image alone challenges the Bible. A transgender woman in a religious pose. . . . Get [*You Got to be Kidding!*] on your Kindle or take it on a trip, the time will fly by—boring this is not!" *Transgenderzone*

"A riotously funny read, I recommend it to anyone who's ever questioned organised religion, especially that of the Bible-bashing, homophobic kind." *Anna, Look!*

"This is hilarious! Joe Wenke gives a nod to Mark Twain as he looks at the Bible with fresh eyes and with the pen of a thinking comic." *Bill Baker*

"This is without a doubt the funniest book I've ever read. I sat with my parents and read aloud some of the passages and we all laughed a lot!" *Emma Charlton, Bookswithemma*

"Very tongue-in-cheek, sarcastic and pointed, dedicated to Christopher Hitchens and Thomas Paine, both of whom would, I believe, really enjoy this book!" *Sarah Hulcey*

"The cover of the book itself is a slap in the face of transphobia. . . . If this book accomplishes one thing, I hope it pushes prejudiced people toward acceptance of LGBT people just as they are." *Isaac James Baker, Reading, Writing & Wine*

"Brave, brilliant and funny. Page after page, biblical chapter after biblical chapter, absurdity after absurdity, this book delivers laugh after laugh. Joe Wenke has crafted the answer to the fundamentalist literal reading of the Bible with the perfect recipe of rationality, candor and humor." *Max Gelt*

"Brilliant . . . for once a funny look at ALL the Bible's insanity." *Jo Bryant*

"Would make a really wicked Christmas present for your Christian friends who have a sense of humor and a sense of the ridiculous." *Ed Buckner, American Atheists*

"Oh my! This is very funny . . . Joe turns everything on its head and makes it a really interesting read." *Stephen Ormsby*

"BEST THING I've READ IN AGES" *Phillip A. Reeves*

"Whether you are an atheist or a Christian who can see the absurdity of some of the anecdotes narrated in Holy Scripture, Joe Wenke's humor won't be wasted on you." *Mina's Bookshelf*

"Great book! Funny and easy to read." *Violets and Tulips*

"Funny and to the point read. Takes a look at the Bible and points out all sorts of inaccuracies, illogical stories and questions. Strongly recommend." *Hertzey*

"Witty and wise. Joe Wenke takes a critical, provocative look at The Bible and he does so with regular hilarity." *Dana Hislop*

"A must-read for anyone who still thinks the Bible is the inviolable word of God — sense of humor mandatory." *K. Sozaeva*

"Such a funny read, my son & I actually read it together! Laughter abounds!" *Rael*

"Deliciously witty!" *Jack Scott*

"Irreverent and hilarious. I am no Bible scholar, but I feel like I have been given the funniest crib notes on this most widely read and probably as widely misunderstood book of all time. I laughed out loud at Wenke's common sense observations and interpretations of this tome." *Lorna Lee*

"Will keep any freethinking reader laughing the whole way through." *George Lichman*

"[*You Got to Be Kidding* is] entertaining and enlightening." *Patti Bray*

"You will be laughing yourself silly while reading this book! In fact, you may find yourself bookmarking a bunch of pages to discuss with your pastor and friends later!" *S. Henke*

"I could not put this book down." *Jackie Hepton*

"This author allows the reader to explore and learn about the Bible with a tongue in cheek attitude that keeps you laughing and turning the pages." *Tricia Schneider*

"Some of it made me feel like I might wind up in hell for reading it, but if you keep an open mind and a light heart, you'll have a blast." *Jon Yost*

"Don't read the Bible! Read this!" *Dr. Dan*

"I'm still laughing." *Paul Wilson*

"GREAT. What hogwash we have been fed. Thanks, Joe." *Colin M. Maybury*

"Unforgiving and hilarious." *Phil*

"This book is so funny." *Crystal*

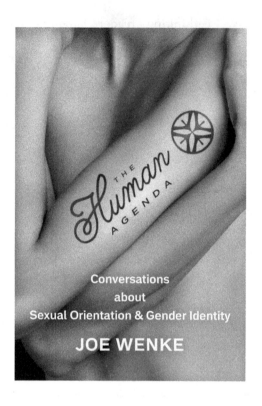

Conversations
about
Sexual Orientation & Gender Identity

JOE WENKE

JOE WENKE'S THE HUMAN AGENDA

In THE HUMAN AGENDA: Conversations About Sexual Orientation & Gender Identity, LGBTQI advocate Joe Wenke speaks with some of the community's leading change agents. In these wide-ranging and probing conversations, amazing people share their personal and professional stories along with their profound commitment to freedom and equality.

GISELE ALICEA (aka Gisele Xtravaganza), *fashion model:* "Transgender people are real people. We have mothers. We have fathers. . . . We have families. We have somewhere that we came from."

ASH BECKHAM, *speaker and advocate:* "It's really hard to not empathize with someone that you have a human connection with."

IAN HARVIE, *comedian:* "It is brave to be yourself."

DR. CARYS MASSARELLA, *emergency physician:* "Being transgender is not biologically hazardous."

CARMEN CARRERA, *performer and fashion model:* "We are one human race. Some women have penises. Some men have vaginas. What's the big deal?"

ELEGANCE BRATTON, *filmmaker:* "There is such a massive gap in understanding between what has been sold as the gay life and what has been the experience of gay people of color."

ANDRE ST. CLAIR, *actor:* "You can refer to me as male or female. As long as you're not doing it disrespectfully, I'll respond."

Y-LOVE, *hip hop artist:* "You can only have unity through diversity. Otherwise, it's just homogeneity."

ANDREW SOLOMON, *author:* "I think there is a tyranny of the norm. . . . But actually what science indicates is that diversity is what strengthens a society or a culture or a species."

Also featuring Kristin Russo, Aidan Key, Hida Viloria, Hina Wong-Kalu, Dr. Jonipher Kupono Kwong and other leading change agents.

THE HUMAN AGENDA addresses some of the most critical issues facing the LGBTQ community, including:

- The marginalization of transgender people

- Breaking down the sexual orientation and gender identity binaries

- The fluidity of sexual orientation and gender identity

- The challenges of coming out

- The religious justification for bigotry against LGBTQI people

- Marriage equality

- The right to adopt children

- The politics of difference: sexual orientation, gender identity and race

- Reclaiming language: the power of "queer"

JOE WENKE'S THE TALK SHOW, A NOVEL

Someone is following Jack Winthrop—most likely the gunman who tried to kill America's most controversial talk show host, Abraham Lincoln Jones. Ever since that fateful night when Jones called Winthrop with his audacious proposal, life has never been the same. Winthrop, an award-winning New York Times reporter who calls the Tit for Tat strip club his second home, agreed to collaborate on Jones' national "Emancipation Tour." The plan is to bring Jones' passion for radical change to the people and transcend television by meeting America face to face. Now Winthrop has to survive long enough to make the tour a reality.

As the reach of his stalker spreads, so does the fear that Winthrop's unconventional family is also in danger—Rita Harvey, the gentle transgender ex-priest and LGBT activist; Slow Mo, the massive vegetarian bouncer; and Donna, stripper and entrepreneurial prodigy—as well as the woman who is claiming his heart, media expert Danielle Jackson.

Steeped in the seamy underbelly of New York City, THE TALK SHOW is a fast-paced and mordantly funny thriller that examines how the forces of nihilism threaten our yearning for love, family and acceptance.

"... It is now a pleasure to read criticism of my work
at the good high level where Mr. Wenke resides."
—NORMAN MAILER on *Mailer's America*

MAILER'S AMERICA
Dr. Joe Wenke

"Essential reading for all who have enjoyed Mailer's work"
—J. MICHAEL LENNON
author of *Norman Mailer: A Double Life*

PRAISE FOR JOE WENKE'S MAILER'S AMERICA

The reissue of Joseph Wenke's thoughtful study, *Mailer's America*,
provides renewed hope for a deeper understanding of Mailer's work.
No other commentator has focused so relentlessly on the deepest
purpose of Mailer's hugely varied oeuvre, namely to "clarify a
nation's vision of itself." Wenke's examination inhabits, patrols and
maps the territory between the millennial promise of America and
its often dispiriting actuality. His study contains probing, nuanced
and careful examinations of all Mailer's work though the mid-
1980s, including one of the first major examinations of Mailer's most
demanding novel, *Ancient Evenings*. Wenke's book deserves a wide
audience, and is essential reading for all who have enjoyed Mailer's
work. — *J. Michael Lennon, author of the authorized biography,
Norman Mailer: A Double Life*

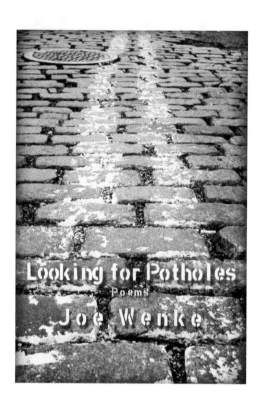

Looking for Potholes

Poems

Joe Wenke

JOE WENKE ON LOOKING FOR POTHOLES
AND FREE AIR

"The poems are very entertaining. Each one is like a little surprise package for the reader to open up. If you enjoy experiencing little epiphanies and revelations about a variety of subjects, including freedom, equality, mortality, troubled relationships, human identity, love and the mysteries of existence, then these poems are for you."

CPSIA information can be obtained
at www.ICGtesting.com
Printed in the USA
LVHW101258040422
715255LV00012B/39